Jumping Problems Solved

Jumping
Problems Solved

CAROL MAILER

WARD LOCK

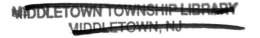

A WARD LOCK BOOK
First published in the UK 1996
by Ward Lock, Wellington House, 125 Strand, LONDON WC2R 0BB

A Cassell Imprint

Distributed in the United States
by Sterling Publishing Co., Inc.
387 Park Avenue South, New York, NY 10016-8810

Distributed in Australia
by Capricorn Link (Australia) Pty Ltd
2/13 Carrington Road, Castle Hill NSW 2154

A British Library Cataloguing in Publication Data block for this book may be
obtained from the British Library

ISBN 0-7063-7394-4

Typeset in Linotron Plantin by Litho Link Ltd, Welshpool, Powys, Wales

Printed and bound in Great Britain by The Bath Press, Avon

All photographs by Bob Atkins

Line illustrations by Eric Apsey

Contents

Acknowledgements

My thanks to:

Margaret Clarke who first introduced me to gridwork; Margaret Millward who carried on the good work; to my father who encourages my ideas and builds the results today.

The models, who were just as keen for the unflattering shots to be included as well as the good ones: Jenny Amos, Araz Baldar, Lesley Bayley, Amanda Brodie, Sarah Elwood, Mary Fuller, Paula Horwood, Teresa Knapp, Brenda Moorhouse, Belinda Neill, Helen Phillips, Samantha Strong, Gemma Truman, Debbie White's lovely grey Charlie.

And very special thanks for being so co-operative and allowing us to take show photos to: Elaine and Peter Kemp, Mr and Mrs Stan Russell, Philip Parren, Keith Dellar; and Mrs Mandy Stibbe for making the whole group of us – models, horses, photographer and me – so very welcome at Waresley Park.

Introduction

There is scarcely a jumping problem for either horse or rider that cannot be solved, or at the least improved, by the careful and methodical use of gridwork. Gridwork, properly introduced into your schooling sessions, cannot fail to improve the ability and competence of horse and rider when jumping, whatever the original standard of the partnership. It will help you both to maximize your potential over fences however basic or inexperienced you may be, and to produce show jumping rounds without stops, runouts or knockdowns. When you are jumping clear rounds happily in competition, more advanced gridwork exercises, using very basic poles and wings, will help give you the extra improvement to excel in a jump-off.

Cross-country riding will also benefit enormously, both from the time element and the safety aspect. Coffins, steps, banks and drops, bounces and combinations: all these will ride far more safely if the horse is neat and nimble in the air, qualities that can certainly be developed on the grid.

Not everyone can be a world beater, but gridwork can and will make you and your horse jump more proficiently, and you need never stop improving. Gridwork will always be able to help you improve, and any difficulties you encounter can be analyzed and resolved.

There are very few jumping problems that cannot be tackled by using carefully prepared grids. Knockdowns, runouts, refusals, lack of confidence both in horse and rider: there are different grids to cure all the problems you are likely to find when jumping. No matter if you or a previous rider has caused the bother, it will be up to you to sort out the problems, and it will help if you have a clear picture of what you hope to achieve.

Most horses and riders can resolve their problems, particularly when jumping, but are you realistic when it comes to your aims and ambitions for your particular partnership? Do you want to win top class BSJA competitions or does a 15cm (1ft) pole look enormous? Can you see yourself competing at Badminton or Burghley three-day-events, or would you be happy to scramble over a small log in the corner of your field? Most riders will be happy to achieve a standard somewhere in the middle, but, of course, a lot will depend on your horse.

A Suitable Horse

Buying a horse with glaring defects in its conformation or temperament may be economical, but will certainly make it more difficult to school on. Gridwork, of course, will help produce improvement in even the most unlikely animal, but it will obviously take more time to be effective.

Weigh up what you want to do: if you want to jump to a reasonable standard, you should choose an animal whose physical make-up does not deter it from being amenable to jumping. Would you choose a good short back, well-placed hocks, sensible head carriage, undamaged legs, good feet, quiet breathing, and a nice bold, sensible eye, or, alternatively, a long back, weak hocks, hollow neck, lumps and bumps and thickened tendons, shallow or boxy feet, sounds like an express train, and a silly eye and expression.

You will not be able to do anything with an unsound horse, so that must be your first priority. In jumping every other physical disadvantage can be greatly improved with gridwork, but unsoundness just gets worse. However tempting it is to buy a horse that is perfect in every other way, if there is the slightest doubt about its ability to remain sound, leave it alone. Have it vetted by a real 'horse' vet, and make sure he or she is perfectly clear about what you want to use it for. They will then be able to advise you about the horse's suitability for all the work you have in mind.

Every horse will have a limit to its ability to perform over jumps, so try to choose a horse that will stay one step ahead of your ambitions. If your ambitions do not match your pocket, you will have to lower your sights. You may well be pleasantly surprised at how much improvement you can make both with a novice or an experienced horse if you work at the correct type of schooling.

Whatever you buy, whatever the problems, however naughty, difficult or misunderstood the horse is, if you want to get the best out of it when jumping, gridwork will give you both all the expertise and discipline required to negotiate the fences willingly and well.

Financial limitations, however deep your pocket, are bound to arise when you buy a horse, but it is worth pointing out that you should try to buy the best you can afford. It certainly will not cost you any more to keep.

ONE

Who needs Gridwork?

This chapter provides an overview of how gridwork can help in the education of horses and riders of all standards, from complete novices to those riders who are already jumping quite sizeable tracks. The problems presented by 'naughty' horses, and how gridwork can help in solving them, are also discussed, as a prelude to the more detailed advice given in later chapters.

The Novice Horse

The term 'novice' can be used to describe horses ranging from one that has never left the ground to one that is already jumping decent coloured tracks easily and is expected to go a lot further in his career: it all depends on your expectations. A horse that would be a real novice to an international rider may be one that has lots of scope and talent and is already showing ability over 1.23m (4ft) fences – such a horse might well be classified by an inexperienced rider as already far more advanced than anything they would be looking for. The definition of a novice can therefore vary, and everyone will have their own ideas of just how much ability a horse has to show before it is a novice no longer.

Despite this, a completely novice horse can be defined as one that has no experience at all of leaving the ground.

Such a horse would be untried and unspoiled, and theoretically, if he is trained properly, all should go smoothly and your horse will rapidly become proficient, when he will no longer be deemed a novice. Unfortunately, of course, so many things can go wrong, however carefully you bring on a novice animal. You will need to be either an exceptionally talented rider, or very lucky, or both, to produce an experienced and proficient animal without shedding some tears somewhere along the line.

Every horse will maintain a different rate of progress. Temperament may dictate how much he will be able to absorb with each schooling session; conformation may affect how much he will be able to achieve before he feels tired. Above all, none of his ability will be realized without the direction of his rider.

Every horse and rider can benefit greatly from working over grids. In fact, gridwork is absolutely essential for both horse and rider to learn to jump and to improve their ability over fences. Then, when they have achieved some sort of proficiency, more advanced gridwork exercises will always be able to assist their technique. It will also help to solve most of the problems that may arise once the horse is out and competing.

Before attempting to jump, the novice horse should be expected to walk, trot

*Let the grid help
develop your horse's
confidence and
jumping expertise.*

and canter obediently on the flat. He should be willing to go forward from the rider's leg, and should accept the signals given through the contact with his bit. For her part, the rider should be able to understand the principles of producing impulsion.

However proficient the partnership is on the flat, the horse will still be a complete novice over poles, so do be prepared to make allowances for his lack of experience. It is unrealistic to expect the novice horse to go out and jump a course of jumps without first having some practical experience in leaving the ground, and if you want to get down to working on the basic principles of jumping, for both yourself and your horse, gridwork is the simplest and most effective way of acquiring the necessary skills.

Gridwork will give the novice horse confidence in his own ability to leave the ground. Carefully introduced poles placed at correct distances should help the horse to develop his technique over small fences, and the positive effect of these very early exercises should not be underestimated. If his introduction to jumping is carefully planned and carried out methodically, the horse will never lose whatever natural ability he has for jumping. Even after a long lay-off, a few times up a familiar grid will be enough to tune him up again, and prepare him to progress further. These skills will stay with the horse for the rest of his life, so you can see how important it is to get it right from the very beginning. If you do get it wrong and confuse him in the early stages, you will only have to backtrack and start again, possibly this time with a less than co-operative horse.

Try to be sensible with your training. If the horse is going exceptionally well,

do not be tempted to go much further than you originally planned for the session. Think of the exercises as a series of plateaux, rather than a peak to be tackled all in one go. Plan to establish the same exercises really well for at least three sessions before moving on to anything more difficult, and if he is not going particularly well on the day on which you planned to advance, stay with the familiar work until he is ready mentally to accept a little more.

You should be aiming to make it easy to produce the maximum effect without too much hassle, and you should also try to make training exercises *fun*. Perseverance and patience will ensure that your horse finds it easy to do what you want at each stage and jumping will be a pleasure for him rather than a penance. In Chapter 4 we will look at grids to make life simple for the novice horse to start off with, and suggest follow-up exercises to increase his scope and ability.

The Novice Rider

As with a novice horse, the ability of a novice rider can vary quite considerably according to who is defining the overall standard. Compared with a Grand Prix dressage rider, most everyday riders would be novices; on the other hand, someone who has been riding for a year should be far more advanced than a complete beginner.

If you are an absolute novice, you should aim to attain some proficiency on the flat before even contemplating jumping. If you start jumping before you are ready, not only will you feel insecure but also by trying to be too ambitious you will adversely affect even the most genuine of schoolmasters. Before

jumping at all, you should be in control at walk, trot and canter, and be able to ride circles comfortably. You should also be keen. A competent instructor and a reasonably well-schooled horse will help the complete beginner to learn far more rapidly and, as in all things, the more time that can be put into learning, the quicker the improvement.

Unless you have serious problems with nervousness, your balance should soon improve to the point where you feel you would like to start jumping. Sensible gridwork, correctly presented, will be

Although small, Jenny's pony, Minnie makes full use of the skills that gridwork has given her to cope easily with the jumps at a show. She very clearly enjoys her jumping.

just the thing to help you get off the ground and develop the skills of balance and technique. However much confidence you have in your own ability, you will be far better starting off jumping simple grids under supervision.

An experienced and willing horse is ideal for starting off a rider over fences, as you will be able to concentrate on your position rather than on producing the horse. Again, a decent instructor will also be invaluable at this stage: if you try to muddle through on your own, you will probably upset both the horse and yourself, and get nowhere. However much it costs, try to set enough aside to pay for this help.

Try to find a trainer who is happy to work with a novice. Some instructors prefer to work with more advanced riders, while others specialize in novices, so make it absolutely clear to the trainer what standard you are at and what you are hoping to achieve. It is vital to be honest at this stage or you will not receive the sort of help that you need, and if you start off along the wrong lines it will cost you far more in tuition to put things right at a later stage. Get the basics firmly established, and then even if you can only afford occasional lessons you will still be able to carry on.

The instructor you choose should be enthusiastic and knowledgeable about the use and positioning of grids. Grids are by far the most effective way of teaching anyone to start jumping, as the sheer repetition of simple exercises will enable an inexperienced rider to get the right feel. Theory is not enough – you must practise to acquire the physical skills necessary to stay in balance and feel secure while the horse is jumping. A competently-skilled and willing schoolmaster taking you through a small grid

will teach you far more about the *feel* of jumping than anything else, especially if there is someone there to help you with any adjustments to your position.

The reason grids are so beneficial is because they both teach and allow you to know more or less what the horse will be doing underneath you. Grids built with novices in mind prepare you for when the next jumping effort will come, so that you can concentrate on feeling in

balance. And of course, you will learn to jump far more quickly if there are four or five jumping efforts in each exercise, rather than trying to get it right over a single obstacle.

In a grid, even if you make a mess of the first element, you will learn to recover your balance over the remaining obstacles, which will stand you in good stead when you want to start competing. The more natural you feel with the horse, the easier it will be for you to be successful in the future, so it is well worth drilling yourself over these small fences until it all feels much more consistently right.

If you really cannot afford professional help, keep your eyes open and approach someone who looks impressive in their jumping to ask for some tips. Most riders will be flattered, but remember: only approach the ones you would like to

Charlie is a super schoolmaster and is popping sweetly through this basic grid, giving Sarah every opportunity to concentrate on her own position.

emulate. Look for a horse and rider at ease with each other, a compatible partnership – in short, the sort of relationship you want with your horse. If they are fighting each other, whichever you may think is at fault, that rider will probably not be the one to ask for advice.

Novice riders will make rapid progress with the diligent use of grids, and in Chapter 3 we will be looking at the most beneficial use of the poles and distances to encourage this improvement.

Naughty Horses

However well brought up a horse may be, occasionally some of them become naughty, particularly when it comes to jumping. Most of the problems are, in fact, caused by the rider, whether it is you or a previous jockey, but sometimes the horse wilfully takes you on and you need to know how best to sort the problems out.

The 'naughtiness' can take many forms. Refusals, runouts, knockdowns, going too fast, going too slow, getting under the jump, standing off too far, napping at a particular obstacle – there are so many ways in which the horse can get the better of you and defy your instructions. However, persistence and gridwork will certainly improve, and probably solve, all the problems and tricks he can throw at you.

The only problem that is really difficult to solve is that of the horse that behaves impeccably at home and waits until you are in a show situation before displaying his naughty side. The only option you have then is to persist with his schooling and his outings. You must just hope that if you drill him enough at home, and *do not* change your style when

you are in a show situation, he may come right with time.

Many horses who do play up at shows are picking up nervous tension from the rider. They feel that the rider is anxious, even though they may have started the original anxiety themselves by behaving quite unpredictably, and this vicious circle will continue until the rider is just as calm and consistent at a show as in their own schooling area.

The repetition of sensible gridwork exercises can only improve the overall relationship between you and your horse as you try to make it easier for him to do what you want. It will also give you more confidence to decide if he is being naughty or is simply confused. A sharp smack may sometimes be necessary, but you must be certain that it is justified. Your gridwork will help you feel what is going wrong underneath you, and whether it is your fault or his.

Good Horses

All horses make the odd mistake – usually because of something lacking in the rider – and gridwork will be the most beneficial way of tuning up the partnership between horse and rider.

However good the horse is, he requires proficiency from the rider to enable him to do his job smoothly and effectively. Many people buy a real schoolmaster, and then forget that they still have to press the right buttons to keep him jumping successfully. Why should the horse go on automatic pilot all the time? He needs the impulsion necessary to keep doing his job properly, and working through grids will help the rider to balance and ride the horse in a way that will make his job easy. Even the very best of horses will give up if they

Opposite: Experienced riders like Belinda know that gridwork will enable their horse to jump cleanly, even if they get a little close on take-off.

find things too difficult, so it is up to the rider to give the horse greater help instead of hindrance.

More Experienced Riders

Experienced riders know why they should use grids as their most effective jumping aid: gridwork has enabled them to help their own horses to fulfil their best potential at whatever standard they may be able to achieve. Obviously every horse cannot be a worldbeater, but it is nice to know that you are competent to bring him up to as high a standard as possible.

Riders with less experience form the largest group of all, and they will benefit greatly from learning how basic gridwork can help to improve themselves and their horses, and make jumping an enjoyable occupation for both. Although these riders may be competent and keen to use gridwork in their schooling, they need to understand which methods of using grids will bring out the best in them, and help them to help their horses. All these aspects are explored in later chapters.

Riders who do not want to know about grids usually end up in a muddle, with all sorts of jumping problems. They expect the horse to do all the work without any help from the rider, instead of the jumping being a joint effort. They do not seem to realize that a little hard work from the rider will pay off by making it so much easier for the horse to do what they want. Any lack of attention to detail in the schooling will usually result in poor performances. The rider will either have to accept this as normal, or end up having to seek professional advice – and more than likely this advice will be to go back to basics and start off properly with gridwork!

TWO

Equipment

Whatever standard you and your horse are at, improving the way the partnership jumps means using equipment.

It would be nice to approach the showjump manufacturers directly and order everything you are ever likely to need to be able to school your horse properly for jumping, but unless you are making a business of schooling showjumpers, it is most unlikely that you will be able, or in fact want, to ever spend this kind of money on ready-made sets of jumps. Constructing jumps at home, on the other hand, need not be horrendously expensive, as there are many alternative ways of making obstacles from bits and pieces. The only criterion should be that they are *safe*. This means jumps should:

★ have no sharp edges or protruding nails

★ be easily displaced but solid in appearance

★ not be too heavy or awkward to be portable

★ have proper wings.

Wings

Consider first whether you are able to afford to buy wood, nuts and bolts, and proper cups, or will have to make do with whatever you can scavenge.

Showjump manufacturers will send out brochures describing their products, usually with the specifications of the wood used. Unless you plan to have shows, or the jumps are going to receive a lot of use, check the measurements of the cheaper wings, usually called 'paddock' standard. You will also need to know the number and length of bolts and how many nails you will require. The diagrams or photographs should tell you everything you need to know.

Do not try to be too elaborate. You do not need massive 1.85m (6ft) BSJA-standard wings to start with, if ever. They are terribly cumbersome and far too heavy to move around, and unnecessarily high. All you need is something workmanlike that will support two or three poles without toppling over – 1.23–1.38m (4ft to 4ft 6in) is an ideal height for schooling, as the wings will not be too heavy to move around. If you are using much flimsier wood than is generally recommended in the brochures, they will also be far more stable if you do not make them too high.

Obviously a pair of wings with both of the uprights the same height will be easier to build than sloping wings. There will be no awkward angles to cut, just straightforward bolting and nailing together. Also, you will be able to drill

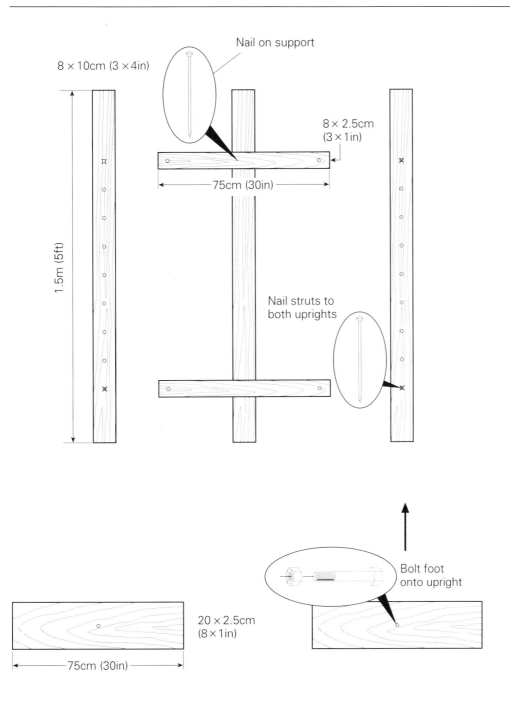

8 × 10cm (3 × 4in)

Nail on support

8 × 2.5cm
(3 × 1in)

75cm (30in)

1.5m (5ft)

Nail struts to
both uprights

Bolt foot
onto upright

20 × 2.5cm
(8 × 1in)

75cm (30in)

cup holes on each side, so three wings can effectively build two jumps (Fig 1).

Finally, you will need to buy cups to support the poles, and it will be wiser not to drill the holes out until you are sure they are in exactly the correct corresponding place for whichever cups you purchase.

Almost anyone should be able to put together this very straightforward design. All you need is a saw, drill, spanner and hammer, plus the materials,

Fig 1 Home-made small wings, ideal for schooling.

and then it is purely a matter of bolting and nailing the cut pieces together. If you really are totally hopeless, however, and have nobody to help you, you will either have to buy ready-made jumps or make do with bits and pieces.

Economizing

Builders' merchants who specialize in supplying wood are an excellent source of raw materials for constructing a serviceable and inexpensive pair of wings. Most merchants will cut the timber to size, which will save hours of strenuous sawing. To economize further use sawn timber instead of planed, and creosote or wood preservative instead of using paint.

Secondhand builders' yards can often supply wood far more cheaply than timber merchants. Even if it is damaged or substandard, it should be adequate for your purposes. They will, however, be unlikely to saw it to size for you, and it might be difficult to find enough similar-sized wood to allow for easy construction. If you happen to be lucky you can save a lot of money, but practically it may be difficult to get exactly what you want. That does not mean that you cannot compromise on your plans; not using the exact size timber will hardly put your horse off, but do be careful that the wood you choose for uprights is going to fit your cups – too wide, and you will not even be able to get a convential cup on the wings, or too narrow, and the cup will tilt on the angle and not support the poles properly.

Horse sales are often useful places to find a source for secondhand jumps. Even if the wings are too expensive, there are often odd cups and other old equipment that you could quite easily renovate yourself.

Poles

Whatever you plan, you must acquire poles. Unless you are prepared to spend money on machined 'proper' jumping poles, look around.

Agricultural merchants will stock fencing posts and rails, and often poles. Specialist sawmills will be much more economical, and you will pay far less for rustic poles that are untreated – they might be thicker at one end than the other, but the horse will not mind.

Find out where other people get their poles. You might be able to buy some older, shabbier poles from a riding stable; check out the ads in horsy magazines and the local papers. You must find some somewhere, because you will not be able to school without them.

Hiring

Often riding centres hire out their facilities by the hour. Perhaps that will be your best option, but do check what you will get for the hiring fee. If the jumps are all stacked in the corner, you will spend at least half your hour setting up the fences.

Using Scrap Materials

Jumps can also be put together using scrap materials. Oil drums, old doors, straw bales and plastic containers (old cooking-oil drums from chip shops are ideal), can all be utilized but avoid anything that has contained chemicals or sprays: you will be asking for trouble if they are left out in the field. You should also check that any old doors or timber you acquire are not painted with a lead-based paint. Lead poisoning, though rare nowadays, is still seen very occasionally.

Carefully stacked supermarket fruit boxes can be useful, although they will not last very long. Bricks can be built in columns to support poles, but you will not be able to have them too high before they topple over.

Plastic sheeting, old fertilizer bags or blue bin liners can be used to simulate water ditches, and with a little effort, you could soon dig out a small dry ditch. It need not be too deep and wide, but just enough to make something that looks quite different.

Hedge cuttings can be used to pack out brush frames, so keep an eye open along the roadside for that sort of work, but do *not* use garden hedging – it might be poisonous, and you never know what fertilizer or chemicals might still be on it.

Old pallets can be dismantled, and each one should provide enough wood to construct a wing. Alternatively, they can be sawn in half and used as fillers.

If you do not have any old paint around the house, buy it from the end-of-line bargains at DIY stores. You will need one or two bright poles for some of the exercises, and even the most tasteless of colours will have the right effect on your horse. The worst colours will probably be left over and so very cheap!

Whatever materials you use, make sure that your jumps will dislodge easily. Do *not* wedge the poles into some sort of upright to make the jump stable: it will not be safe. Remember also to check for sharp edges or protruding nails; you are trying to improve your horse, and not to maim it.

If you have to make do with a complete hotchpotch of scrap materials, do not be downhearted or discouraged. As long as your grids are built at the correct distances, and you are able to simulate some of the ideas, you will manage.

The Jumping Area

When you set up your jumps, try to arrange them in a specific area. If you can, use a purpose-built arena; it will probably be dressage sized, that is 20m by 40m or 60m. This is ideal for the early stages, but you will need extra room for the more advanced work.

If you have a field to work in, try to set up your grids to utilize the fence. Novice riders and horses will feel safer with one side secure. Jumps set in the middle of a field are fine and save a lot of time moving the grid around, but you must be confident about your steering. You will be able to approach the fences from either rein without changing the jumps.

Mark out a sensible area to work in and try to stay within the boundaries to encourage a disciplined approach from both you and your horse.

Once all your equipment is organized, you can make a start.

The horse does not seem to mind this scrappy jump at all!

THREE

The Novice Rider

It will be very difficult to improve a horse, novice or experienced, unless you know more or less what to do. If you are a novice rider, gridwork will bring you up to a recognizable standard more easily and in a shorter time than any other method of learning to jump, but how do you start?

Trainer and Schoolmaster

If you have never tried to jump before, you will need some help, both from a decent trainer and an experienced horse. However difficult it is to arrange, you will learn far more quickly and with a better chance of getting it right.

If your own horse has no experience of jumping, it would be very easy for you both to develop bad habits. It would be far better for those potential bad habits to remain dormant. There will be plenty of time and more opportunity to develop them later along the way, and develop them you surely will without the right sort of help.

Do not start off along the wrong lines and confuse your horse. At some stage you will have to start to do it properly, and it will be far better to be taught the basic principles on a horse who will be pleased to help you learn correctly. If you are a complete beginner at jumping, it is also much more economically sound to start off in the right way. Otherwise, at some stage in the near future you are going to have to pay far more heavily to be put back on the right track.

An experienced horse, particularly one who is used to novice riders, will know his job inside out. You will be able to concentrate on what you alone should be doing instead of worrying about producing the horse correctly, too. In addition, novice riders need to build up confidence carefully, not under pressure to go too far too quickly. They must acquire a feel for the balance, rhythm, contact and degree of leg necessary for the schoolmaster horse to be able to jump easily and efficiently, and only then will they be in a strong position to help a novice horse.

An understanding of how best to produce a horse for jumping is essential. Although there is no substitute for the physical experience of actually getting a horse in the air, it does help to recognize the sort of feel you need on approach, take-off and landing to make it *easy* for the horse to do what you want. Most of the refusals and disobediences at fences are because a horse has arrived at the fence and is physically unable to jump because he is lacking the necessary impulsion to do so.

Theory

Reading will help you to understand the principles involved in jumping horses. You will discover that your horse needs controlled and controllable energy from impulsion, rhythm and balance in his paces, and an agreeable temperament to perform well for you.

Impulsion equates with power. Your horse must be working with his hind legs well underneath him, otherwise he will lack the power and spring to jump easily. You must learn to ask for this power by using your leg consistently to produce forward movement, and contain this forward movement with a steady and consistent contact on the reins.

If either your leg or contact are not working properly, the horse will be lacking the vital power or impulsion necessary to produce a good jump.

Maximum impulsion is produced by asking with the right degree of strength of your leg aids into the right degree of strength of contact with the horse's mouth, and you will only discover the correct feel to produce impulsion by practising this technique under know-ledgeable and experienced supervision.

Once you have established a more consistent feel of impulsion, you need to maintain it in rhythm. Every stride should be bouncy and active, neither speeding up nor slowing down.

You will also read about keeping your weight well down into the stirrup and through a flexible knee, and how you should not look down at the fence you want to jump, but up and forward where you mean to go.

The theory is very easy to absorb, and understanding it will certainly be of immense value, but at the end of the day you must sit on the horse and practise – and practise and practise – until you feel

you have got it right. This must be the *right* feeling, which will stay with you constantly throughout the whole of your jumping endeavours.

First Steps

Do not start trying to jump until you feel reasonably secure and in control in canter. Even if you feel safe enough in trot, your first jumps are literally going to be elevated canter strides for your horse, and you must feel confident. Get the feeling right.

There is an excellent exercise to help you produce the secure and well-balanced position necessary over fences before you actually leave the ground. Shorten the stirrups from your normal length by one or two holes. Think about condensing your body down through all its hinges: the waist, hips, knees and ankles. You will then feel slightly more exaggerated angles than at your normal length of stirrup. The idea is for your lower body to act as a shock absorber for the movement of the horse and allow the upper half to remain balanced. Enough flexibility through the ankle, knee and hip will only come with practise, and you must learn to think *down* rather than thinking forward.

Now try to hold this position in trot. Instead of rising or sitting, let your weight hang down into the stirrup and absorb the trot motion through the joints. Your upper half should be as still as possible. If you can trot 'standing up' like this for half a dozen strides, you will be in the optimum position for going over jumps – but no cheating! Hanging on by the reins is not OK; neither is bumping back down in the saddle.

Use a neckstrap to start with. Hang on to the neckstrap and let it help you begin

Brenda's use of her leg, coupled with a good contact give Millie power and spring to spare.

3

4

If you can hang in balance at trot, then you can hang in balance over a fence.

to get the right feel. Your horse will go smoothly if your hands are quiet and the contact consistently comes from the same place. Let your weight drop as deeply into your stirrups as you can. Encourage your knee and hip joints to be as flexible as possible, to act as a shock absorber to allow your upper body to fold and follow the movement of the horse. If you are too far forward you will be pushing yourself back off his neck. If you do not have enough give through your knee, you will fall back on to the saddle again.

This exercise is not as easy as it sounds. You might manage well for one or two strides, but it is difficult to keep it up for seven or eight. Persist until you can – it will help you develop the best position to be in over a jump without the added complication of jumping first. If you can 'hang' in balance in trot, you

will find it is the perfect place to be over a fence. You will feel comfortable, your hand will be light and consistent, and your horse will find it much easier to operate underneath you.

This is a marvellous exercise for more experienced riders, too. If you have started to feel a little out of balance in the air, do this trotting exercise. It will remind you of where you should be over a jump, and how it should feel. If you have been getting too far forward in the air and collapsing, this exercise will get you hanging back off the stirrup bars again. If you have been left behind, it will probably be because of a stiff knee and hip; trotting standing up will loosen up the joints and help you regain your flexibility to fold in balance again. Reminding yourself how it should be done will do you no harm at all.

Experienced or novice, this exercise will only reaffirm how to produce the position you should be striving to attain in the air. The novice rider will find it extremely beneficial to do this before starting jumping in any form. When you can do this consistently without falling either way out of balance, you are ready to start jumping.

Starting with Canter Poles

Try to work in an enclosed area, primarily to give you confidence and keep you safe. It will also make you a little more disciplined in your work if you do not have too much space to ride round at first.

Start with a line of five placing poles at canter distance, around 3.35–3.7m (11–12ft) between each pole (Fig 2). This is another reason why you need help: if the distance is not quite right for your horse, you will not be experienced enough to know. Your instructor will be able to see that the poles are set at the most beneficial distance to make it as smooth as possible for you.

Trot down the line, trying already to ignore the poles, looking up and away, and riding into a consistent, light contact. Then repeat this in canter. You will feel a slight elevation over each pole.

Remember the trot exercise and float your seat slightly, with your weight down into the stirrups. Use your neckstrap to help you stay in position without hanging on by the reins. If you can get this right, you do not need to exaggerate and change position when the jumps are built: you will simply need to stay in the 'up' part of the float a little longer while you are in the air. Concentrate on letting your weight drop as deeply as possible through your knee and down into your

stirrups, and try to keep your weight hanging there throughout the whole of the exercise.

If you are on a nice experienced horse, you will not need to worry too much about your steering, only your balance. He will be genuine and try to help you. A novice riding a novice will only be wondering if the horse is going to be spoilt in the process.

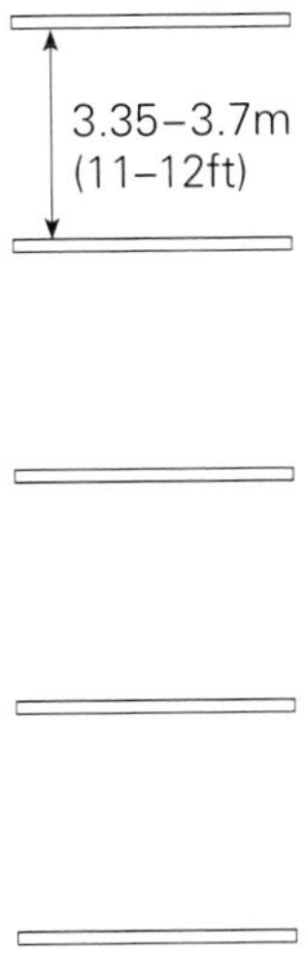

The First Jump

When you are comfortable over the poles, make the last one into a low cross, about 23cm (9in) high in the middle (Fig 3). Come in canter, look up, let your horse do it for you and let your knee absorb the feel of the jump. Do not forget the neckstrap: it will help your hands to be in the right place, and keep you securely in balance as the horse comes up and jumps.

You know when he is going to jump because it will be exactly in the same place as the fifth canter pole. There are no surprises coming, just a slightly different feel from the horse as he elevates. Do not change position from the one you have been trying to get in the standing trot. Just because you are leaving the ground, it does not mean that you should be doing anything different. Go with the horse and enjoy the feeling.

Repeat the exercise until you are completely happy and confident with it, landing in balance and cantering on a few strides after the cross. If it feels comfortable, you have got it right. If it feels a bit jerky and you land at odds with the horse, keep practising. Be patient: once you have got this feeling right, you will never need to change it, whatever you jump. The difficult part is reproducing it perfectly all the time!

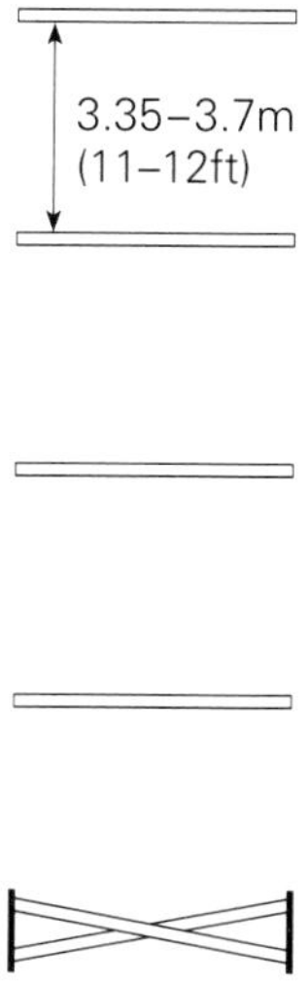

3.35–3.7m (11–12ft)

Fig 2

3.35–3.7m (11–12ft)

Fig 3

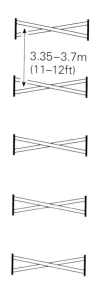

3.35–3.7m
(11–12ft)

Fig 4

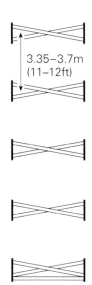

3.35–3.7m
(11–12ft)

Fig 5

A Small Grid

When you are comfortable and not landing in a heap, gradually build all the canter poles up into small crosses (Fig 4). This will give you five chances in a row to practise absorbing the elevated feel the horse is giving you. Concentrate all the time on looking up where you are going and keeping your balance.

This is why it is so important to try to learn on an experienced horse. You have more than enough to think about in producing your own position, let alone teaching a horse at the same time. A novice horse really needs to be produced from trot, which at this stage would not be so comfortable for you as canter. In a nice floating canter, you are almost in the right position to jump anyway – all you should be feeling is an exaggeration of the movement.

Until you are completely comfortable and confident, do not allow yourself to be pushed any further. Approach in a nice active canter, thinking of letting your weight go deep into the stirrups through a relaxed knee. Keep the neckstrap and use it, but try to retain a slight feel on the contact too. As you gain confidence and it starts to feel right more consistently, you can let go of the neckstrap. If you let go prematurely and you are not balanced enough, you will catch the horse in the mouth. There is nothing wrong in hanging on to the strap – even much more experienced riders get hold of a handful of mane if they are in trouble.

Practise hard to be in balance over these crosses. Get them right and there will be nothing to prevent you being absolutely fine as the jumps go up. Your position should *not* alter; only the timing of that position in the air will need adjusting. Over a larger jump the horse

is going to make more effort and spend a bit longer in the air. *Your balance will need to adjust in timing, not position.* Get the timing right, and you will be set up for anything you want to tackle in the future – but you must get it *right*.

Feel the rhythm the horse produces down the grid. Concentrate on looking up and away. Let the neckstrap help your hands to be in a more consistent and sympathetic position – it will help your wrists and elbows be more flexible to allow for the movement of the jump with your body. If you feel a little stiff and rigid above the waist, try to relax and allow your shoulders, wrists and elbows to absorb the motion. You need a bit of flow as much as the horse does.

The only way you will learn to jump is by repeating the exercises until they feel right. Theory is fine, and can help you get into some sort of organized position, but you have simply got to *do* it to gain any sort of improvement. However, do not put yourself under too much pressure. Enjoy what you are doing. This might be as much as you are able to absorb in a first session, so do not try to extend yourself to do too much if you begin to tire. You need to be well in control of your balance for the next step.

Increasing the Grid

Now make the last jump a bit bigger, by putting a horizontal pole behind the cross (Fig 5). All the way through the grid, concentrate on riding in the *same* way as before, to capture the same feeling. Do not change things and disturb the rhythm because the last jump is bigger. It is your horse that is going to need to make more effort, not you.

Stay calm, and plan to remain in position in the air a touch longer and absorb the slightly more exaggerated feel through your knee. If you can prevent yourself from wanting to 'go' to the fence with your hands and body at this stage, it will save you an awful lot of remedial work later on.

Do *not* try to assume a different position. The one you are already comfortable with over the crosses is fine; just hold it a little longer in the air, allowing the extra time for your horse to be over the fence. You should not feel much difference as he jumps. If you do, go back and repeat the previous stage a few times before trying it again.

The whole point of using the grid is that it will make you relaxed and familiar with what you want to do. Keep the first jump very small, to encourage your horse in smoothly. Once in the grid, the jumps will reproduce the same striding every time. You will be able to judge when your horse is going to make his effort, and be prepared for it to happen underneath you. You will have the chance to practise producing a rhythm over several jumps in a line rather than just one, so obviously you will improve!

Do not give yourself too much to absorb. If you think the jump at the end looks imposing, reduce it. It is not meant to be a test: it should bring you on, not put you off. Trying to get it right will be much easier for you in the future if you let it all happen in simple stages.

When you are relaxed about the whole thing, raise the middle cross to make a small upright (Fig 6). Feel and absorb any difference in the action. The only change should again be in the timing, not in the position in the air. After a bigger effort from your horse, try to land yourself through a nice soft knee. It will help your balance tremendously if you keep looking up.

When you are happy with this, put a horizontal pole, not very high, behind the first cross (Fig 7). Take care to adjust the distance between jumps to remain at 3.35–3.7m (11–12ft). Now you might feel your horse adjust his stride a little more. A schoolmaster will be clever enough to do it smoothly, and help you stay in balance. A novice horse would need a more experienced rider with the right attitude to keep him confidently coming to the fence with absolutely no interference whatsoever.

If you are not in balance because the horse has taken off unexpectedly, you will know from practice how the rest of the grid should feel. Try to recapture the comfortable feeling of the rhythm on the way through.

If you have got in front of the horse and are hanging round his ears, you have looked down. Your eye has encouraged you to try to arrange yourself into your jumping position instead of waiting to feel him actually taking off. If you are left behind, the neckstrap will help you catch him up again on the way through. Get the *feel* of what is happening underneath you – do not look down to try to see. It will not work, and will be a very difficult habit to lose.

If you keep getting this wrong, you must start to approach in trot. Whether the horse's stride is short, long or perfect, you will not be able to see when you think he is going to take off – you will have to feel it. Because the trot stride is only half the length of the canter, your horse will find it easier to adjust to the jumps. There is also far less chance of being a long way out from the best take-off point. If he misjudges in trot, it will only be by a matter of 60–90cm (2–3ft). In canter, it could be as much as 1.54–1.85m (5–6ft), making quite a

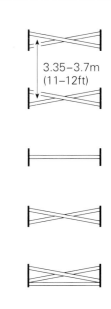

3.35–3.7m (11–12ft)

Fig 6

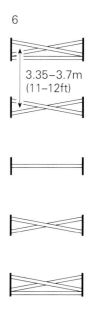

3.35–3.7m (11–12ft)

Fig 7

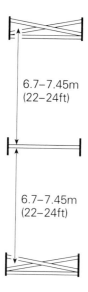

Fig 8

6.7–7.45m (22–24ft)

6.7–7.45m (22–24ft)

Fig 9

10.15–11m (33–36ft)

10.15–11m (33–36ft)

difference to the effort needed to get over the jump. This is one of the reasons why a novice horse should start jumping from trot: there is far less scope for error, even if the rider is totally out of balance.

This is also another reason why you should start jumping on a horse who knows how to do it nicely. Two novices together may well confuse each other, neither of you being in a position to help the other. A novice horse needs the right sort of help, and unless the rider knows how to provide it, the horse will be unable to cope. You could put him off completely, simply by failing to recognize just how much impulsion he requires. At least if you start off as a passenger, you will discover how it should feel to do it correctly. Even if you then have to get back on a novice horse, you will know what sort of feeling you are trying to reproduce.

An experienced horse will allow you to start in canter. It will be much easier for you, as the jumps will simply feel like an extra-large canter stride. Canter through the grid, taking the original position you practised when standing in trot. This floating, more flexible seat will make it relatively straightforward to adjust your weight and balance over the fences, especially if you use a neckstrap. It is purely commonsense to use one to keep you safe and secure without hanging on to the horse's mouth, and you will be able to keep your hands quiet in the air. The more you practise, the safer it feels.

Your weight dropping into the stirrups will help to keep your balance. The more secure your base is, the easier it will be for your body to fold into the most comfortable and correct position in the air. Do not be tempted to hurry along too quickly. If you dispense with the neckstrap too soon you will occasionally

hurt the horse's mouth, and even the most genuine schoolmaster will resent this and eventually become unwilling.

A Basic Combination

Practise over this simple grid until you find it easy. When you are totally happy and holding your balance consistently, remove the two cross poles so that you are left with three small jumps with one stride between each of them (Fig 8).

There will be a slight change in your horse's rhythm. He will no longer have to go quite so high between the fences, and will make a more normal stride. Feel how to adjust to this: the non-jumping strides must not be ridden from a 'droopy' position. Sit up, look away into the distance, keep a light, consistent contact and ride your horse's canter.

Do not collapse just because the small cross poles have gone. Think about getting your weight deep into the stirrup and a little less forward before folding again for the next effort. Looking up is the best aid for this. It will help prevent you being sloppy on the non-jumping stride, just by encouraging you to look where you are going.

The jumps will again be different in their timing. Feel how to adjust to the lower, non-jumping strides and the corresponding extra effort over the jumps. If the rhythm and balance is right, it will be comfortable.

Do not rush things through. Change the grid gradually and absorb how the different exercises feel before altering any more.

There are many variations on this plain grid. You can lengthen the distance out to 10–11m (33–36ft) to give you two non-jumping strides between fences (Fig 9). Practise feeling the new rhythm

this produces; change it back again. Anything which makes you *feel* what is happening will be good for you. Increase the size only if you want to: do not allow yourself to be persuaded to jump bigger fences until *you* feel ready.

Attitude and Experience

Once you have learned how to feel balanced and comfortable in the air without needing the neckstrap, you should be more or less in a correct position. Just check that you are not keeping yourself secure by hanging on by the reins. If it *feels* a good position, it probably *is* good.

The most important thing of all to remember in future is not to alter this feeling. Once your position is OK, do

If it helps your confidence through this basic combination, leave canter poles down in place of the small crosses until you feel totally happy.

not change it. If you are right over a 60cm (2ft) pole, the *same* position will be just as right when held over a 1.53m (5ft) parallel – you would just need to hold it a bit longer. The timing changes, *not* the overall method.

If you have help to get your position and the feel of jumping a fence correctly right from the beginning, you will make rapid progress. You will be governed only by your confidence and the scope of your horse. Do not be too demanding and self critical: you will not capture the right feeling immediately. When you do, at first it will be erratic.

You will not learn to feel simply by theorizing. Repetition and perseverance over familiar obstacles is the only correct way to develop the balance and rhythm necessary to be in a position to produce a horse nicely over fences.

Without expert help, you really should not contemplate starting off with a complete novice horse. It is just asking too much of both of you. If your horse is a complete novice and there is no option, try to get an experienced rider to start him off. Learning together would be far from ideal. The pitfalls involved in such a venture are enormous, and will have far-reaching consequences.

Single Fences

Do not change your jumping position when moving away from the grid. Once the grid has enabled you to get a feel for jumping, you can start popping over single fences. Position them along the wall or fence to help with the steering and do not be too ambitious with the size. If you overface yourself you will have to retreat, probably several stages, so be careful. A trainer will be a far better judge of your progress than you

are, and should not allow you to get into a position where you will harm yourself or your horse.

There is always the most enormous temptation to look down just as you approach a new jump, and it is almost impossible to resist. Do try! You will progress far more steadily by feel than vision, and your balance will not be disturbed by what you think you can see. Do *not* look for the take-off point: let your horse make up his own mind. If you prepare yourself to jump by looking for a stride and you get it wrong, you will be so out of balance that your horse will be upset too.

Just concentrate on keeping everything as smooth as possible. Allow your horse to get on with it and go with him. Do not get ahead of him by trying to organize his stride. If you do not distract him, he will manage much better in choosing his own stride. If you want to help rather than hinder, do not wriggle about. Apply more leg to help his impulsion, and do not try to organize anything else.

Progress to jumping single fences from turns, as well as the familiar lines. The grids suggested for the novice horse (see Chapter 4) will help the novice rider too, and will be particularly beneficial if ridden on a more experienced animal. The feeling over a fence that your gridwork has produced must stay with you. As you progress and begin to ride courses, keep that feeling. How you have learned to feel on the grid is how you should feel over any fence, wherever it is.

The gridwork will always be able to help you as well as your horse, whether it is a novice or experienced. If things start to go wrong, you will know how to cure them. Go straight back to the grid!

FOUR

The Novice Horse

The best way to solve jumping problems is not to allow them to arise in the very first place.

A novice horse that has not done any previous jumping at all provides the ideal opportunity for teaching him to jump without encountering any of the hang-ups or physical difficulties a much more experienced animal might have developed. Prevention is far better than any cure, and nowhere is this more applicable than in teaching novice horses to jump *without* problems.

The way to develop his ability over fences is full of potential hazards. Get it right, and you will find that most of the major upsets can be avoided. Get it wrong, and every time you ask for something different or requiring more effort, your horse will at best say 'Perhaps', and at worst 'No'.

Riders will find that a methodical approach to the horse's early training, using mostly common sense, will give him the confidence to do what you ask. This should ensure that any problems which arise will be minimal, and should be corrected easily by retreating a step or two in the training schedule. Repetitive and carefully planned exercises can be designed to bring on novice horses by giving them confidence in their own ability to cope with whatever is in front of them, so it is absolutely essential that

the rider does not become too ambitious too quickly. The horse must have the chance to absorb and become familiar with whatever he is being taught *before* moving on to the next stage. Remember that if things go badly because of a lack of forethought, the horse will absorb that as well, and instead of gaining greater confidence he will lose whatever he had already acquired. Of course, there are bound to be hiccups, but if you combine patience and persistence with sensible gridwork, you should not come across any major problems.

Mental and Physical Approach

You should aim to make it mentally easy for your horse to understand what is expected of him, and physically easy by providing him with enough impulsion for him to do the job you are asking for. Most horses thoroughly enjoy jumping, and even if your horse does not have the potential scope to be a superstar, you owe it to him to give him the necessary skills to develop fully whatever ability he already possesses.

Even if he is somewhat limited, either by temperament or by conformation, he will still be able to jump something. A silly nature and lack of concentration makes jumping mentally more difficult for the horse than a calm temperament and a willingness to listen to the rider. Long backs and weak hocks make it physically more difficult for the horse to get sufficient impulsion to find jumping quite as easy as a short-backed, active horse, who overtracks more naturally. However your horse is put together, though, both mentally and physically, you will still be able to use the same methods of gridwork in his schooling.

It may take the less advantaged horses more time to develop their skills, but it will work. The sheer repetition of the exercises will encourage the silly horse to concentrate totally, and any physical weaknesses will be improved as the exercises gradually build up more strength and general co-ordination in the working parts. Gridwork will help every horse improve, especially if you have already tried to start him off using other methods which have not always been particularly successful.

Aims and Consistency

You may not be looking to produce a world beater – riding club and local jumping competitions are quite testing enough for the average horse and rider – but whatever level you are aiming at, you want your horse to do his best. If you can give him the confidence and competence from day one, life will be so much more pleasant for your partnership in the future.

Of course, it will help the horse if your balance is good and you know what you are meant to be doing and feeling. An experienced rider would definitely be a preferable choice for introducing a novice horse to his first few schooling sessions over poles. The horse will find it easier to concentrate on what he is meant to be doing if the signals are clear and consistent, and consistency is very important in gaining the novice horse's confidence. If the rider's approach to the grid keeps changing, then the horse will be confused. Help your horse, do not hinder him.

Unfortunately, sometimes it will just not be an option to start your horse off with every advantage that goes with an experienced and competent rider. Such a rider might not be available or affordable, so you must do the best you possibly can.

If you are a complete novice you will find that the exercises suggested will help you as much as your horse. But not on him! Even if you own your own horse, go to a riding school to learn. You will be given a horse to ride who knows the job so well that he will not be distracted or put off jumping by any acrobatics from the rider. Do not try to get away with false economies. You *must* invest in a few lessons so that at least you know the sort of feeling you are trying to create for your novice.

Even experienced riders use a neckstrap on a novice horse, so do not think it is babyish. It is an essential piece of equipment for enabling the novice rider to jump without damaging the horse by catching it in the mouth. It will also possibly save you from falling off if you lose your balance, and it will certainly make the whole job more comfortable if you can hang on to something secure.

Being inexperienced does not have to be an insurmountable barrier to starting off a horse jumping, but it can be a severe handicap. You must have help from someone on the ground who knows how to prevent you making a mess of it. Confidence is a very fragile commodity –

difficult to build and frighteningly easy to lose, particularly when your horse is involved as well, and it is the novice horse who needs every consideration so that his introduction to jumping is completely enjoyable.

Essential Help

Before you go as far as starting a schooling session over jumps, whether you are a novice or experienced rider, do enlist the help of somebody on the ground. You might fall off, so they will be there to help in that aspect, but more importantly you will need someone there to help move the poles. It is absolutely hopeless to have to get on and off between exercises. You will completely lose any feeling of continuity and rhythm in your approaches, and a good rhythm around your schooling area is essential.

You need to keep coming to the poles with impulsion, so that at whatever point on his stride the horse meets the pole he can adjust easily from the strength of your rhythm, even in walk. This is really when you need the most help, so if you can manage to have someone on the ground who knows what they are doing, preferably an experienced instructor, your horse will make rapid progress through these early stages.

If your helper is not particularly horsy, they should still manage to set the poles how you want them if you tell them clearly. Just make sure you know what you should be setting up, and in order to set the poles at the correct distances for your particular horse, do use a tape measure. If you want the distance between elements to be 3m (10ft), make sure it is, and not wavering somewhere between 2.75m (9ft) and 3.35m (11ft). You are just wasting time and confusing the horse if you set the poles wrong.

Once you are more used to setting up the grids, learn and practise pacing the distances. You will be pleasantly surprised how easy it is to adjust your own paces to coincide with the distances you want to set. Use the following guide:

★ Four short paces equal 3m (10ft)

★ Lengthen a little for 3.35m (11ft)

★ Stretch a bit for 3.7m (12ft)

Then practise! It depends on how long your legs are, but it certainly will not take long to recognize what sort of pace you need to take to exactly equal a metre or a yard.

The average horse needs to cope with double and treble combinations set at around 7.45–8m (24–26ft) and all the early schooling should reflect what you will be asked to cope with in later competitions. Then, when you are in the ring, you will know if a particular distance in a combination obstacle will suit your horse or not. It is handy to know whether to push more, or be a little steadier on the non-jumping strides.

If you are working in an arena or an enclosed area, you can mark up the distances on the fence or wall. Then you will not have to rely on guesswork until you are able to pace out the distance correctly. Mark the wall accurately and use the marks to help you, and again, practise pacing these distances until you are confident that you can do it accurately. It is no good trying to use the distances suggested here if you do not set them up properly.

Starting from Scratch

We have already covered all of the practicalities of making jumps from bits

If your horse questions you at the single pole, do not turn away: just keep asking until you get co-operation.

and pieces, so let us make a start and see what the very first jump is going to be for your novice horse: he is going to start off with poles on the ground.

One pole is fine to start with, and it is unlikely that you will encounter much resistance. However, if the horse does regard the pole as an unsurmountable barrier, be prepared to teach him a very valuable lesson: to go forward from the rider's leg. You *know* he can step over a pole on the ground, so make him!

It would be very difficult for you to ride him so badly that it would be your fault that he refuses, so do not feel inadequate if you have to be unsympathetic with him. However long it takes, hold him into position facing the pole. Do not let him turn away. Nag away with your leg, and do not let him choose to do anything other than go forward.

Look up, look away, and do not let your eye be drawn to the pole. As soon as your eye drops to the pole, there will be an unconscious inclination of your weight and a corresponding 'giving' in the contact. Then, because you have

'changed the rules' immediately in front of an obstacle, your horse will detect this straightaway and wonder what the problem is. If you just keep pushing with your leg into a nice consistent contact and do not look down, he should not even think to question you.

It is the horse that actually has to negotiate a jump, and he will be able to concentrate far better if you do not distract him by altering your style in the last second before take-off.

Most of the problems of refusals later on will be caused by your looking down and giving away the contact just in front of the jump, so it would be nice if you could start to brainwash yourself not to look down in the early stages of your horse's jumping career. Looking up, looking away: it is such a good habit to get into, even at this early stage.

When you start to jump courses, you will need to ride a track and look ahead to see where you should be going. It will not be very helpful if you miscalculate a turn because you are looking down to see what your horse is doing, rather than

feeling what is happening underneath you. Plan all your horse's schooling, even walking over a single pole, with a view to preventing problems later on. It will certainly save you frustration and expense in the future, so do try to lay good foundations.

If your horse does question you, do not be too perturbed. Whatever methods you employ to encourage him, you cannot afford at this stage to let him choose to argue. Insist on him going over, however long it takes. If you were facing a baby horse at a big jump and it said no, then it would be perfectly understandable. But a pole on the ground presents no physical stress, only a mental block, so overcome this right from the start. If you have to be led, fine! Do not worry. He *will* get the confidence to do it, however anxious he is, because you mean to persist.

Once your horse is happily walking, trotting and cantering over a single pole, and it is really most unlikely that you will have a problem with this, then you can add another pole.

★ A long-striding horse should have a distance of 3.7–4m (12–13ft)

★ An average 15–16hh horse will be comfortable with a distance of 3.35–3.7m (11–12ft), and a shorter-striding or small animal with 3–3.35m (10–11ft)

★ Big ponies can cope easily with distances between 2.75m and 3m (9ft and 10ft), but be prepared to reduce the spacing further if the pony is much smaller in height.

You are looking for the horse to walk three paces between poles, trot two paces and canter one. So: the horse should walk over the poles with alternate front legs leading at each pole, trot with the same leg leading at each pole (and do not be alarmed if this produces a slight feel of a 'hop'), and canter with the same leg leading all the way through.

It is easy to see at walk if the distance is correct for your particular horse. He needs to meet the pole so that it is in the middle of his stride. Get the distance set so that he neither lengthens his stride to try to reach the other side, nor shortens it because he is getting too close. If he starts to lengthen his stride as his confidence grows, you can alter the distance correspondingly. In the early stages you do not want to be catching him out, and a nice sympathetic approach to make it easy for him will work very well.

Do not forget, you *must* do this pole work on both reins, and if possible, use both rustic and coloured poles. If your horse gets used to both types of pole when they are on the ground, he will be far more amenable to jumping both types of obstacle when they are larger. It would be most inadvisable to use only rustics for pole work, then change to colours for his first proper jump. However well he has been behaving, it is taking an unnecessary chance and might produce a problem which so easily could have been avoided. If he had not already been introduced to colours on the ground, he could be quite forgiven for spooking, and you will not be sure if he is being silly because there is a different obstacle or just a change in poles. Even if it is inconvenient to move the various poles around, do help your horse to have the confidence of familiarity when making his first real jump.

The First 'Real' Fence
When the horse is working happily over five poles in walk, trot and canter, he will be ready for his first real jump. This will be a small cross pole.

Set the cross in place of the last ground pole, so that the middle is around 23cm (9in) high (see diagram on page 27). Approach in trot down the familiar line of poles, look up, look away

and keep your leg pushing into a nice consistent contact. If he jumps, fine! If he lifts his legs higher, and stays in trot over the cross, fine! If he stops, not fine!

Do not try to analyze why he has stopped at that moment. You can think about that once he is over. It is probably your fault for changing the style as you anticipate something different, but at this precise moment you need action, not theory. The jump will be small enough for you to insist that he steps over it: do not let him turn away. If he really will not budge, get your helper to lower the poles to the ground, remembering to remove the cups, and then insist on him going forward.

Again, it must be stressed that it is very unlikely that you will find a problem with this. If you do, back off, get him going confidently over the two poles placed close together, and only gradually raise the ends to form a small cross. This is another of the reasons why you need a good helper, as you may have to repeat the process on the other rein. It would be almost impossible to manage if you were on your own.

Increasing the Grid
When the horse is happily trotting down the line of poles and over the cross – and it really does not matter if he is staying in trot or actually popping – make a cross in place of the middle pole. Again, this is most unlikely to cause a problem, but if it does you know what to do. Insist on him stepping over the cross, even if it has to be lowered, and if he is being silly, just make sure that you do not let him duck out over the last cross. He is already familiar with that one, so do not let him be naughty for no reason at all. If he is inclined to dive to the side, be ready for

this and keep him absolutely straight.

Usually, this type of naughtiness is preceded by an increase in pace, so be aware and do not let him accelerate as he goes through the grid. Once he feels he might be in control of the speed, he will think he is up to deciding what else he can do, and if you give him a choice of options he will always choose the wrong one – at least as far as your own wishes are concerned!

You must concentrate hard to get these early exercises right. Just as you may allow your horse to develop bad habits, either through inexperience or impatience, so you can also get him into the habit of behaving properly and accepting with good grace whatever you want him to do. If you are looking up and forward and keeping hold, that is maintaining a consistent and supportive contact, your steering should be fine.

It is also possible that your horse is enjoying his jumping so much that he might do an extravagant leap over the first cross. This could easily unbalance you, so do keep your weight firmly into the stirrup and do not let yourself tip too far forward in anticipation. You want to produce as smooth a jump as possible, and even if he is going extra high, he will settle down after a few efforts as he discovers that this is unnecessary.

If the horse is jumping and not just trotting over the crosses, the ground pole between the crosses should produce a nice rounded canter stride. Do not remove the pole, as it will help him balance himself, and will also steady him if he shows an inclination to rush.

If all is well, then you can make a cross at the first pole. Again, if the previous exercises have gone smoothly, there is no reason to suppose he will find three in a row particularly difficult. And of course, you are only going to give him the third cross when he is totally happy with the other two. If it gives you more confidence, you can add a placing pole in front of the first cross at the same distance you have been using. If the horse is rushing at the line, it will help to steady him up, but if all is going smoothly, it will not hurt to approach the first cross without one.

It is nice if the horse approaches in a smooth and rhythmic trot, pops the first cross, canters through the grid without blundering on the poles, and comes out in a calm canter on the correct leg. So how can you make sure he does?

If your horse stays in trot throughout, merely lifting his legs higher over the crosses, do not try to hurry him and bully him actually to jump. He is going forward, negotiating the poles, and, as far as he can tell, doing as you ask. Do not get impatient if it is not quite what you want from him. This is something that he needs to learn for himself, and he will only be able to do so if you give him confidence from your leg into a nice consistent contact.

Consistency from the rider is essential to enable the horse to concentrate on what he is doing. He does not need the distraction of your trying to make him jump. Give him impulsion and let him sort it out for himself. If you try to help him too much he will lack confidence in his own ability. When the situation arises when you need him to help you – and it will – he will not have the confidence in his own ability to cope.

Patience must be at a premium as you keep re-presenting him to the grid. Do not try to rush and canter in so that he is forced to jump. He will only become confused and mistake what you are asking for. Eventually it will dawn on him that it will be easier to do a little pop over the cross instead of elevating his legs, and you will find that the poles on the ground will encourage him to stay in canter through the whole exercise.

Encouraging a Proper Jump

It is possible, though very unlikely, that your horse manages so well by staying in trot that you feel he will never actually decide to jump.

Using the third cross, raise the ends of the poles so that the angle of the cross is more acute. The actual height of the obstacle will hardly be increased, but it will look much more imposing, and will encourage the horse to jump instead of remaining in trot. Be very careful that you do not frighten him by increasing the severity too much too quickly. A gradual increase will probably produce the required effect, but do not upset him in case he decides he does not want to do it at all. Be prepared to decrease the cross again until he is confident once more, and try a different approach.

Give him a lead with an experienced horse, and hope that he will imitate the expert. This will almost certainly do the trick, as he will be anxious not to be left behind. As soon as he is jumping the crosses happily behind his friend, send him round on his own. Do not worry if he reverts to trot again. He will now know how to jump when the need arises and the cross gets bigger.

Once he is happily doing what you want, then you can allow him to canter, but even at this very early stage, do not let him rush. At the slightest hint of an increase in pace, go back to trot.

Do not be perturbed if you do not get as far as this with your first session. Always use your common sense, and do not pressurize the horse to do more if he is getting tired. It is vital to his mental state, as well as yours, to finish on a good note. If he finds the work too demanding because he is tired or just not quite ready, you will do more harm than good. Conserve his energy and goodwill for the next session.

Consolidating your Work

However well the horse has gone, do not start the next schooling session where you left off. Go back to the ground poles and work your way up over the small crosses. If you have worked wisely on the previous occasion, everything will go smoothly, and you will soon be jumping the three crosses.

Just make sure that familiarity with the work does not encourage him to start one or two little tricks that could possibly develop into something more serious if left uncorrected. Be alert to him hanging one way or the other as he goes through the grid: this might lead to runouts in the future. The appearance of the crosses should help him to keep straight down the middle, but they will not be big enough to enforce this. Keep the contact and steering positive.

Do not anticipate the turn after the grid, either. Your shoulders should be level as you leave the grid, and you must ride the horse straight for at least three or four strides before you turn. A collapsed shoulder will indicate that you are leaning in and allowing the horse to just fall in round the corner, losing impulsion, which is not very helpful when you are jumping a course. So many problems in the ring are caused by the horse anticipating a turn and losing impulsion, so do not let him acquire this habit. A little care and attention, even in such basic early stages, will prevent so many difficulties arising later on.

Because you should have reached this point with far fewer trips down the grid than in the previous session, your horse will have plenty of energy left to do a little more. However, if he is hesitant, do not rush him. Be resigned to repeating the same work over and over so that his confidence can grow. Do not proceed with anything else until he is totally happy. If he is you can start to add to the grid he is already familiar with.

The novice horse does not want any surprises, so do not be too ambitious. Add a horizontal pole behind the last cross, at a height just above the centre point of the cross and a spread of about 60cm (2ft). Approach the grid in trot. If he canters through, fine; if he wants to stay in trot, do not worry. As long as he goes forward, he will cope. He should scarcely notice the extra pole as he pops over. If he has been one to prefer to stay in trot, this extra dimension will usually encourage him to jump instead.

When you have repeated this exercise happily in trot on both reins, add a similar horizontal pole to the first cross. Do not forget that you will need to adjust the distances so that the non-jumping strides remain constant. It is so easy to forget and add poles to the far side of the first jump without altering the placement of the wings. It would be very difficult for your horse to be asked suddenly to cope with a non-jumping stride 60 cm (2ft) shorter than he is getting used to.

When your horse is doing this quite happily, you can put up the cross in the middle to form a small upright, the same height as the back poles of jumps one and three, and pop him through that. Leave a pole on the ground slightly in front of the horizontal pole which will

then act as a general groundline.

Do this in trot on both reins, and if all is well, allow him to approach in canter. If he rushes, go back to trot. If he prefers to stay in trot on the approach, fine. Do not hurry him and put him under too much pressure too soon. He will be more or less pressed by the size of the jumps and the placement of the ground poles to canter once he is over the very first jump.

If he is going well, do not ask any more on this particular day. However small the fences may be now, you are already establishing the basics of jumping combination obstacles (see diagram on page 30). When you are out competing, you will find that doubles and trebles cause more faults and problems than any other fence, and if you can make it easy for your horse to feel he can cope with a line of fences at this very early point in his jumping career, you are less likely to have him say 'I can't' or, even worse, 'I won't' when he gets in the ring.

Changing the Grid

Ask for more progress only when the horse is totally happy and confident with what he is doing.

Do not change your methods of warming up. Start with the poles on the ground and build up methodically to the stage where you last left off. If you have done these earlier stages properly, you should find he is going well enough to change the grid after each approach.

When the horse is happily popping the three small jumps, make the last jump into a small ascending parallel. Do not have the back pole any higher than it was before: just make the front pole horizontal and far lower. This will be the first

time that you have radically altered the way the grid looks to the horse. Although you may have gone through the stages very diligently, this new 'look' may just cause your horse to lose his concentration and peek at the last jump. Make sure your leg is there a little more strongly to overcome this tendency. Do not hurry, but just be prepared to use a little more encouragement if necessary.

Of course, it might go as smoothly as every other exercise, but if your horse has been at all suspicious about the grid in the earlier stages, this will certainly make him think. If he is really worried and refuses to go, make sure it is not your riding that has caused the problem. Just because the last jump looks a little more imposing, you must not let it affect the way you present the horse. If he senses that you might be expecting some trouble, he will lose confidence in you, and then you will end up in a muddle. So:

★ Do not over-ride and get more speed instead of more impulsion

★ Do not tip forwards on the approach

★ Do not try to produce impulsion with the body and hands

★ Do not look down.

You should know your horse by now. If he has been at all silly at the earlier exercises, however carefully presented, and if you are sure he is going to be silly now, then let this knowledge work *for* you: use more leg but not a faster pace. This is the only difference in your riding that will be effective to overcome his silliness – anything else you do simply will not work! You must stay calm, and present him to the grid at the same speed but with more leg.

If you tip forward on the approach you will drop your hands slightly and the horse will feel this and immediately be suspicious. However much leg you are using will be wasted if you allow the impulsion to disappear through your dropped contact. Stoking him up by wriggling and shoving with your upper body will only distract and unbalance him, and if you look down this again will produce a loss of balance and contact.

Retreat may be necessary. If you reach an impasse, and the horse simply will not go forward from your leg, retreat a stage with the exercise and return the jump to the original cross and small back pole. Get his confidence right back by popping down this grid until you are both happy again. If he has become really upset you may need to go back even further, but this is most unlikely. The usual sticking point, if there is one, is when you change the cross pole to form the small parallel.

When you are ready to try the parallel again, build it smaller, but make sure it still has a similar appearance. It can even be small enough to step right over if necessary, although it is doubtful if you will have to retreat quite so far. Patience and perseverance are once again at a premium, and if it takes you more than one practice session to get him doing this happily, do not worry. He will learn more than enough about co-operation and obedience from your not giving up to make the whole problem almost a worthwhile exercise in itself.

Do not be tempted to miss out on this stage if your horse is being silly. At some stage in his career he is going to tell you 'No', and it will be far better for you to be armed with the knowledge that he is being difficult rather than just lacking ability. You will know for certain that the

jump is not too big for him, as he has already been cheerfully jumping fences of a similar size.

Facing a novice horse to a larger fence without the correct preparation would reflect very badly on the rider's overall judgement, and the horse would be blameless if he refused. The rider would then not know for certain who was at fault. But to a small jump at the end of a familiar grid? Even if the jump has changed in appearance, and of course this is what will cause the problem, you will know for sure that he has the scope

Opposite and above: Cyril is definitely suspicious when the last jump becomes a small parallel, but Teresa has enough strength of leg to overcome his spooking.

to do it, and you will have the confidence in yourself to insist.

The methodical use of gridwork is a major benefit to both you and your horse. If things go wrong, it is simple just to retreat a stage or two until you both regain your confidence. If the earlier exercises have been done correctly, there should be no major catastrophes. If the same steps have been followed each time, the familiarity of it all will make it so easy for you both to be well prepared before trying a little more.

Working on Both Reins

Every time you alter the grid, you should approach it on both reins. If you are working along a wall or fence, this can involve a lot of building and shifting the jumps around. You can see why help from someone already on the ground is invaluable: it will take them long enough to reorganize the poles, so just imagine how long it would take you on your own to do it properly, especially with a horse hanging off one arm.

Do not be tempted to skimp or adapt the exercises because of the manual labour involved. Even if you have to circle away while the grid is rearranged, a helper will give you the opportunity to keep coming in a rhythm, letting the horse settle and take the jumps happily in his stride.

If there is absolutely no chance of help, then you must just make the best of it, and in this case it will be easier if you are working in the middle of an area. You will be able to approach on either rein without changing the grid to allow for a different direction after each exercise is accomplished, and you will only have to get off to alter the jumps, not turn the grid round.

However tedious it is, and however rickety or precariously placed your poles are, you must do this work in sequence, and if it takes you longer to build, hard luck! Just make sure that when you get on after rearranging the grid, that you re-establish your rhythm and impulsion again before you approach.

If you do keep approaching from the same end, even on either rein, do alter the grid round before your next session so that you tackle it from a different way. Leave the placing pole in front of the grid if you like, but it will be more for your confidence than his. Without a pole to rely on he will start to balance himself as long as you ride him consistently. You must not try to help him too much as you approach the take-off point, but give him the impulsion to decide for himself which stride will suit him best. Keep hold, look away, do not look down at the poles, and keep the leg on into a consistent contact.

Do not try to see what he is doing; you must feel what is happening underneath you, and ride him accordingly. If he is slowing down or losing impulsion, use more leg. If he is rushing, adjust the weight and the contact. Work hard to feel that the balance is right between the degree of leg to the contact to produce the maximum impulsion.

Introducing Bounce Fences

When your horse is happily jumping down a line of three fences with no hesitation, signs of clumsiness or rattling the poles you can introduce him to something a little different.

Still using the grid he is now familiar with, one at a time make the placing poles into small crosses so that he will actually be bouncing down the line. This ability to be active and bouncy will be very valuable for both his showjumping and cross country. It is a very rare cross-country course that does not have a bounce in it somewhere, and steps, alternatives at corners, and all kinds of drop will be much easier for him to tackle if he has done this sort of athletic exercise from the beginning. It will also make him a lot sharper in opening his shoulders and bringing his hind legs through actively, otherwise he will start to hit the poles.

Early Carelessness

What if your horse does show signs of carelessness? Even at this very early stage, it would be sensible to let him know that blundering through the jumps is unacceptable. So many horses can jump beautifully, yet spoil their rounds with careless knockdowns. Obviously, it will usually be your fault if your horse does hit a pole, but why should he bother to make the effort to clear the jump if he does not understand that you do not like it?

Each time you hear him touch a pole, let him know that he is wrong. Growl at him. A sharp 'Hey!' is usually enough to make him pay attention. After all, presumably you would shout at him if he bit or kicked at you? Keep him right on his toes and anxious to avoid your grumbling. It certainly would not be too much to ask for him to get used to picking his feet up with a bit more effort. Many horses are very sensitive to even a hint of criticism, so hopefully a yell in his ear will be adequate, and very much kinder than some of the disgraceful behaviour to be seen at shows after a rider has incurred faults. Yanking on the reins, and misusing the whip and/or spurs once they have left the ring, can even be seen at Hickstead or Wembley, and riders of that calibre *do* know better.

Five-fence Grids

When you start building up to five obstacles in a row, do remember the methodical approach. If the horse finds it difficult to cope as soon as the ground poles become crosses, retreat a little and make them smaller. Build up gradually, never losing sight of the object of the exercise, and encouraging his ability to develop confidently with absolutely no undue pressure.

Once he is happy with this, take the small crosses away, leaving the three original small jumps with no placing poles at all. He will notice that they have gone! Changing the grid like this will be just as eyecatching as making cross poles into parallels, so do make sure that you are staying well in balance on the two non-jumping strides. If you look down, you will tip slightly forward and drop the contact, your leg will not be effective, and you stand a good chance of running out of impulsion when you need it most – in the middle of the grid!

All the earlier work should come to your rescue if you feel your horse hesitate as he wonders where the poles are. Do not look to see exactly what is happening, but concentrate on feeling what is going on underneath you. Then, if you feel him peek and hesitate, your leg can instantaneously send stronger signals to go forward.

It is most unlikely that this particular exercise will upset him and make him grind to a halt, but be ready. Horses see things in so many different ways, and even the calmest of horses can take a dislike to the unfamiliar.

The Time Factor

So, you have done as much as you can using the three grid jumps, and your horse is very relaxed, popping the jumps easily and trying hard to pick his feet up cleanly. How long has it taken?

The time taken for each horse to be thoroughly at ease with the gridwork so far will vary considerably. Some horses breeze through all the exercises very competently in just a few days. Others will be slower, needing much longer between sessions to absorb what they have learned.

You will be able to regulate your own horse's pace by judging his aptitude for remembering the previous exercises. It is therefore vital not to change the method of schooling by skipping some of the steps, as this is the only sure way of judging if your horse is mentally and physically capable of moving on. However long it takes, you *will* reach the point where you are ready for the next step. Just do not be too impatient.

Single Fences

Once your horse is completely happy with his grid of coloured and rustic poles, you can plan to introduce him to single fences with fillers.

If you have been working in the middle of an area, your steering should be well practised, but it will still be better to start the horse's first efforts over 'proper' jumps with a wall or fence to help guide him. If this is just not practical, remember that you must be well alert to the possibility of his trying to run out. However relaxed he has been about his jumping so far, he will still be surprised when he sees something entirely different, and so far he will not have seen fillers. It is not a good idea to use them in grids, in case things go wrong and he gets them tangled round his legs. Poles alone are plenty to cope with when the horse is just a beginner, and are less likely to damage or upset him if he makes mistakes. When he is blasé over coloured and rustic poles, you can plan to introduce him gently to something a little more startling.

Approach all these new fences in trot. If he is wrong footed in trot, he will only be 60–90cm (2–3ft) adrift of the most beneficial take-off point. In canter, if he makes the wrong decision about his original take-off he can be as much as 1.85–2.15m (6–7ft) out, making it very difficult for him to jump comfortably. In addition, you will be far less likely to anticipate a trot stride into a jump, and it will be much easier for you to maintain the rhythm and balance necessary for maximum impulsion if you are not looking for a stride.

Common-sense starter

An ideal starter fence can be built with the blocks off a wall, as they can be arranged to be small enough literally to walk over if necessary. Use a wing to guide the horse to the jump, approach in trot, and expect him to do it for you! If all the preparatory work has been done correctly, he should not even hesitate. If he is inclined to be silly, then however much work you have done already he might still play up at the idea of doing something fresh. This is why it is so essential to present a novice horse to something tiny. Just as you have done from the beginning, insist on him getting to the other side without turning away. There is to be no option for him but to go forward, and your new jump is certainly small enough to step over. It would be surprising to meet much

resistance, even with a silly horse, as his earlier experiences will have got him into the habit of doing as he is told.

But of course, *you* must get it right as well. Just because you are doing something different, do not let it affect the way you ride. The general method of producing impulsion and co-operation that your horse has become accustomed to must not change. If you send him different and unusual signals, he will immediately become suspicious and anxious, with a corresponding drop in his confidence.

Brainwash yourself to ride the new jump using exactly the same technique that you have been employing with the grid. Do not forget that if you gawk at the fence, so will he. Unless you look up and away, your body weight and contact will alter, you will lose impulsion, and your horse will genuinely find it difficult to perform properly.

Once the horse is happily popping over your tiny wall, add a pole or another row of bricks. You should only be asking him to jump around 45cm (18in) high, lower than the jumps on the grid, so you know he is up to it. If you do have problems, it will then be because your technique has altered or your horse is being silly, not because he is overfaced.

If you do not gawk at a new fence, neither will your horse.

Additional fences

When your horse is quite relaxed with the jump on both reins, and not until, you may add another jump, preferably similar in appearance 6.45m (21ft) in front of your small wall. If you do not have many fillers, poles will do instead, as the object of the exercise is to produce the confidence in him to tackle two separate and unfamiliar obstacles in a row. The distance is deliberately on the short side to encourage the horse to take just one stride. If he props a bit in the middle, you do not want him to find it difficult to reach the second element.

Remember: when you add a fence, always put it in front of the jump he is already familiar with. You do not want him spooking at the far fence because it is new, and losing concentration. It would then be all too easy for him to crash the first obstacle because he is so distracted.

As he grows in confidence, gradually move the jump out to the conventional 7.45–7.7m (24–25ft) one-stride distance. It is never too early to be practising what you are going to meet in the ring. If he is too confident, making up more ground in the middle and getting too close, put a placing pole in the middle of the distance to steady him. It is much better to use a pole to help the stride at this stage rather than to check with a stronger contact.

Further changes

Your horse will soon discover that there are no particular hazards in jumping two different fences, so you can start to think about adding more variety and changing the rein.

Leave your double along the long side of your schooling area, and plan to introduce a completely new fence set on the

diagonal. Build your new jump using
different materials if possible, and aim to
introduce him to this new obstacle with
the same attention to detail. The fillers
must be lower than the height he is happy
and confident over; around 45cm (18in)
high would be ideal. It would be most
unfair to the novice horse to try to
increase the size of the obstacle at the
same time as changing the appearance
and the line of approach.

Start with a cross pole, and use the
fillers on either side of the wings as an
extra guide. The cross must be small
enough just to step over if necessary.
Your horse might not like the look of the
new jump, but if you have diligently
gone through the earlier stages, you
should be able to insist on him going
forward. Remember, turning away is *not*
an option.

Once he is happily popping over the
cross, make the jump into a small
upright, only about 30cm (1ft) high.
Again, ride him over the fence, using
your leg into a nice consistent contact. If
you look down at the jump as you
approach, so will he, and he will be far
more suspicious of something new if he
picks up any anxiety from you. You have
done all the preparatory work, so do not
let something fresh make you ride
quite differently.

Gradually raise the height of the
upright until it is 5–8cm (2–3in) above
the top of the filler. Your horse should be

Opposite and right: Barnaby lands and
looks surprised to find another jump so
soon, even though he is already
familiar with the obstacle. Mary sends
him forward from an 'up' position,
giving Barnaby all the confidence he
needs to tackle the second fence well.

relaxed enough by now to start moving the fillers in, little by little, until they meet in the middle. Progression depends on your horse's attitude. If he is calm and sensible, four or five moves until the fillers meet should be plenty. If he is silly, it may take ages. If he does take a violent dislike to the fillers, move them out again until he is happy, then start to return them very gradually towards the middle. With perseverance and a patient attitude, you should prevail.

Starting to Ride a Course

It depends entirely on your horse how far you can go with this new exercise. Two such fences, set one on either diagonal, would be ideal to get the maximum benefit from this work. Plan to approach your fences in trot.

It will also help if you can mark out the approximate size of a dressage arena (40 × 20m) in which to begin work. It certainly is not essential, and bigger and sprawlier horses could actually do with a bit more width, but if you try to stay in this sort of area it will guarantee a little more discipline for both of you. Then you can keep coming round on a figure of eight, with your helper gradually altering each fence before you come to it again.

When your horse is happily doing his figure of eight in a nice rhythm over two small uprights, change the direction and the jumps, so that you approach them from the opposite way. Encourage the horse into your outside rein as you turn to each jump – you do not want him to learn to lean on the corners and lose impulsion.

If he does start to anticipate the turn and approach, put a marker in each

Opposite, top:
Barnaby is not allowed to turn away from this odd-looking fence.

Opposite, bottom:
He soon gives in and pops over easily.

Above:
Barnaby shows no loss of confidence as the fillers gradually close in.

corner to ride round. You need to approach these diagonal fences fair and square at right angles and without hurrying, so use anything which helps. You should be looking up and towards the corner of your working area, and trying hard to keep your weight deep into the stirrups and your shoulders level as you land. The horse will immediately detect the slightest tendency of the rider to collapse inwards in anticipation of the turn, and will be only too willing to collapse as well. Trying to keep your shoulders level is the simplest way of ensuring that you do not lean. As soon as you have landed, be aware of riding the horse straight away from the jump. You should be looking for at least three straight strides before you turn. You only want him to turn when *you* ask for it, not because he is deciding for himself. It will not take him long to catch on to where you are meant to be going, and he will not see the necessity of taking the longer route when he can be either lazy or keen and cut the corner.

Keep a very consistent contact with the new outside hand as you guide him round with your inner rein: it is not like when you are riding a bike, where your hands compensate for each other as you steer. Ride your turns so that he is up underneath you, with his neck in a vertical position in front of you. If he leans, you will find it very difficult to maintain your impulsion around the corner and into the next fence, simply because his hind legs are not far enough underneath him.

However long it takes, get this part of the exercise right; it will be immensely important to you in the future. Later on, when you are tackling courses, your horse must be obedient. He will not know which will be the next jump, and if you allow him to fall in and anticipate the turn too much, you will simply be unable to get in line for the next fence. Apart from your becoming unbalanced and losing impulsion, the angle to the next fence may be too difficult to negotiate, especially if you are fighting each other, so do the 'baby' thing and use markers to help you ensure that this little habit has no chance to develop. Even at these very early stages in your horse's career, you can already be practising aspects in training that will be very important in the future.

When he is happy with the new jumps, and you are happy with the balance and steering, you can incorporate your double and grid to make up a sequence (Fig 10). Remember to ride the correct line away from each jump, not allowing your horse to collapse on the corners. The more you practise riding a diagonal approach from a consistent outside hand, the easier it will become for both of you to arrive at the jumps with maximum impulsion to do the job properly. Look up and away into the corners, not down, as you approach each jump, and make sure that your steering signals are clear enough not to be misconstrued. If he lands in correct canter, allow him to canter on for a few more strides before steadying down to trot again.

Do *not* aim for a time factor when introducing new jumps. Each horse will absorb his training at a different rate, and you must be very careful not to miss out any stages in this methodical approach. You will only confuse your horse if you try to hurry through the exercises, and if things go wrong you will have to retreat several stages instead of just one to regain his confidence or obedient attitude.

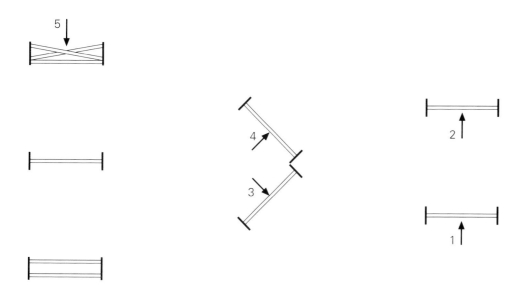

Introducing doubles

When he is happily going over single diagonal fences, and you are entirely happy with your presentation and steering, you can begin to make them into doubles. Use exactly the same method of introducing these new fences as you did with the original grid and first double; *always* build the new fence in front of the jump he is already familiar with, and do not be tempted to rush.

Start with the cross poles set low, then make a horizontal pole before moving the fillers in. You do not need to hurry through this stage, however blasé the horse is. It will only take a few minutes to organize setting up the new jumps anyway, so you might just as well tackle them at each stage of building.

When the horse is happy with this new figure of eight, do not forget to turn the jumps round so that he is asked to approach both doubles from each direction. If your original double along the side is constructed to be jumped both ways, you will be able to use these six small fences with the grid to form an uncomplicated and flowing course (Fig 11).

What if the addition of the extra two fences causes problems? Using the methodical approach to introducing the new jumps should have worked perfectly well, and the horse should not be nervous about their appearance, but there are other hazards involved when riding diagonal lines over more than one jump – most commonly an inclination to run out at the second element. You *know* he is not frightened. After all, he has jumped this fence numerous times as a single obstacle, so he is well familiar with it. So what are you doing wrong?

Check the obvious first. Is the jump builder being fair? Are the jumps perfectly in line, or is there an angle caused by incorrect measuring? Use the tape measure to make sure that the distance between the jumps is the same at both ends. If the distance from corresponding wing to wing is different, then you are creating an unnecessary hazard and actively encouraging an angled approach to the second element.

Fig 10 Starter tracks. Ride a figure of eight over fences 3 and 4 until your horse is confident, then tackle the whole course.

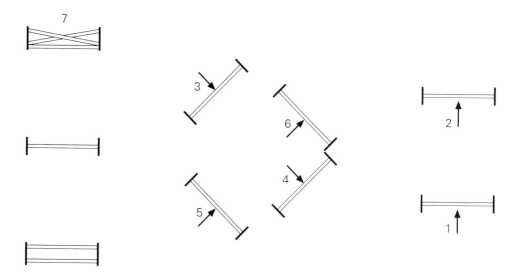

Fig 11 Can you steer? Fences 4 and 6 will act as extra wings to help prevent runouts.

When you want to take a jump on an angle, it should be because you plan to do so, not because the jump builder has got it wrong. Use your common sense in construction.

So your jump is perfectly square. Are the faces of both jumps a similar size? It is not very helpful to jump a wide fence first and then have to carry on to one that is narrower, so again, do be sensible with your construction.

Is the steering accurate? It is so easy to come off the corner looking only to the middle of the first element, and the slightest deviation from the correct right-angled approach will throw you out for the second part. As you turn into the corner, you should already be sighting on the double. Do not allow the horse to fall in round the corner. Push him well up into your outside contact and keep him coming round until you can sight up the middle of both elements of the double. Only when you can see that the middle of both jumps is in line should you straighten up for your approach, and then remember how to ride: shoulders should be level, with no tipping, consistent contact. Keep looking up, look beyond the middle of the second element, and use your leg into contact on the non-jumping stride.

Be positive! If you land in a heap yourself after the first jump, you will drop your hands, lose the contact, and your horse will not know where to go. Given a choice of direction, he will usually choose the wrong way, as it will be the line of least resistance, so your balance must be good enough to allow you to keep riding him in the proper direction. If you have ridden badly, or the horse is going to be naughty, he will usually hang to the outside, so if you are aware of this, take positive steps with your steering to overcome any such tendency. It is also possible to arrange the jumps so that one of them will act as an extra wing on the difficult side.

If your horse is being very naughty, and pretending he cannot jump two in a row, reduce the size of both jumps so that he can actually step over them from a standstill. Then do so, slowly – do not let naughty habits develop. Once he has stepped over the first jump, stay in walk.

You will then have plenty of time to hold him straight for the second. Walk him in to the second jump and kick him over it. Do it again several times: he will soon get fed up with saying 'I won't', and you know that he should not be saying 'I can't' because he has already jumped it before. A very positive attitude and lots of leg should see you quickly past the naughty stage.

Do not think about increasing the size of the jumps again until the horse has obediently negotiated both parts of the double several times in walk. When you are sure you are going to be sharp enough with your steering, send him on in trot. It is essential to land in balance after the first jump to establish the necessary impulsion and steering required immediately, so make sure you are not going to be the cause of any more trouble. If your setback has made you lose confidence in yourself, go back to the straightforward grid that you are both totally familiar with until you feel competent again. If the horse is being naughty, this will make exactly the right impression on him, correcting him methodically and re-establishing his willingness to go where he is asked.

Running out is usually caused or allowed by rider error, particularly if the horse has been going well. Even riders who are very experienced in jumping can sometimes think 'Good boy' and relax too much: an attitude problem can cause just as much bother as a novice rider being physically limited in ability to co-ordinate the aids. Both may result in the horse arriving right at the jump with insufficient impulsion and guidance, so who would blame him for choosing the easier route? It is so very easy when he has successfully repeated the exercise to relax and take your horse for granted, and think he will do it all for you.

Never forget that the horse is doing as you ask because you keep giving him impulsion and directing him where to go. If you fail in either, it just is not fair to expect him to sort it out for you. Why should he jump either a single fence or a double if he arrives at the jump with no impulsion and poor steering? He will physically be unable to cope, however small the jumps. Of course, the horse may sometimes be naughty, but if you have prepared him methodically step by step, the blame for any failure can usually be placed firmly with the rider.

Establishing Confidence and Obedience

Work over these six fences and the grid until you and your horse are happy and confident with each other. If you have more jumps, gradually introduce them to the horse so that he becomes familiar with different obstacles. Increase the size of the fences only when you feel ready, and then only gradually.

There is no point in overfacing either of you, so do not be in too much of a hurry to go out to shows. Try some non-competitive outings until you discover how both of you are going to react away from home. Perhaps you can use the jumping facilities at a local riding school, or hire a purpose-built jumping arena for an hour. Even going over a friend's jumps in a different field will be good experience and help prepare you to jump in competition.

It would be nice for everything to go smoothly once you start competing, but you are bound to find something or other going wrong occasionally. On the other hand, there will always be a grid to help you sort it out!

FIVE

Refusals and Remedies

Refusals are so annoying, especially when they mar an otherwise perfectly faultless round.

So why do they happen?

Causes

There are a number of reasons why a horse may refuse to jump.

Disobedience

Blatant disobedience is a very real problem, and you will have to be very determined and positive to cure this. It is likely that you will have to be prepared to use a stick, and the discipline of gridwork will ensure that if you do need to smack your horse, it will have a constructive effect.

Loss of confidence

A frightened horse is not a naughty horse, but any refusals must still be cured.

A genuine loss of confidence can make even the sweetest-natured and most co-operative horse refuse. Perhaps he has misjudged a spread fence and landed on the back pole, hurting himself. Or perhaps you have flapped going into a jump, using speed but no impulsion on the approach, so that he blundered through it, again causing him much pain.

If he has had to make a supreme effort to struggle over a jump, he will be anxious about the next obstacle and will be halfway to stopping before you get there. Even more damage will be done if he crashes into a jump when refusing, as he will be far less inclined to try again.

Maybe the horse has jumped a big track successfully, but found the effort a bit too much for him to sustain, so that he might try to avoid doing this on the next round.

Perhaps you have jumped him on bad going. If the ground is wet and slippery, he may feel insecure and not want to leave the ground, or if the going is hard, he may be anxious about jarring himself. Set your grid where you know the going is consistently good, and if the ground becomes boggy or too hard, postpone your schooling session. Studs in his shoes will help your horse feel more secure as he takes off and lands, both on slippery or hard going, but it will take some time and practice to rebuild his confidence. Your horse will only become consistently co-operative again when he is happy that the circumstances are safe.

Are you sensible about the number of occasions your horse is expected to perform? He might just be thoroughly fed up with jumping too often and have decided he has had enough. Although this has the same effect as the naughty horse – refusals – the reasons behind his refusing may be different. Until you are aware of the causes of the problem, you will not be able to cure it. In these circumstances, give the horse a complete rest or change of work, and when he does start work again, let him enjoy himself with the easier work on the grid. It will help bring his attitude back in line with how you would like him to behave. And do not do too much in future!

Physical causes

If your horse has suddenly started to refuse after previously going well, check his physical well-being. Is he throwing a splint? Does his back hurt? Does his saddle pinch? Are his teeth distracting him? Is his mouth damaged? So many things that are totally unconnected with behavioural problems can stop a horse, and if it hurts, how else can he tell you except by protesting?

Remedies

Exactly the same sort of gridwork as described in Chapters 3 and 4 will benefit the anxious horse, as well as the naughty horse, and you will find that his confidence will rapidly improve again.

First of all, decide what is causing the problem, and then set about remedying it – with gridwork. In every circumstance except physical discomfort, working methodically over the same type of grid will get your horse going again. Look for consistency in your schooling, so that your presentation to every jump is beneficial.

Responsibility for refusals

The responsibility for nearly every refusal can be placed firmly on the shoulders of the rider. Obviously a naughty and nappy horse may be 100 per cent to blame for stopping, or

refusing even to go near a jump, and if the current rider has done nothing to cause this behavioural problem, she need not feel responsible, but this tendency to refuse or be uncooperative was probably caused originally by another person's poor riding.

Whoever started the trouble in the first place, you will need some help to cure it. Use exactly the same gridwork and method whether your horse is just plain naughty, or has had every reason to justify his reluctance to jump. Naughty horses will take longer to learn to behave, and must be treated with a very bracing attitude. Be prepared for several fairly major arguments at first.

Horses who have lost confidence should still be treated firmly, but with sympathetic undertones. You will be trying to help them enjoy the job again, and once they start to regain their confidence, their progress through the grid will be rapid. Do not be tempted to miss out any of the stages. They are all suggested for a good reason: to get you jumping happily again!

Loose schooling

Most horses enjoy jumping as long as they are not overfaced. Loose schooling, where the horse is encouraged to jump on its own, will show just how willing the horse is. It does not take long for them to enter into the spirit of the game; sometimes they can even be difficult to stop, choosing to carry on round the school and continue jumping without any encouragement. So, unless you have an extremely difficult animal, he should be amenable – as long as you ask correctly.

Admit your own shortcomings

If a horse is presented to a jump with no impulsion, why should he make an

Below:
No impulsion equals a
refusal.

Opposite:
Gemma is determined
not to make the same
mistake again, and
approaches for the
second time in a 'stay
back' position. It may
be exaggerated, but at
least it is effective!

enormous effort to struggle out over it? It is just not fair on the horse, and until you are honest enough to admit that you are the one in error, no improvement will be possible. Admittedly, it is very frustrating to find your horse stopping, but until you recognize and accept that you are the cause, you will not be able to cure him.

Even if the fault has originally been caused by a previous rider, do not expect the horse to recognize that you are quite different. He will only begin to appreciate the change if the new rider presents him to his fences in a way that will make it easy for him to do the job.

So often a rider will tell her instructor 'He doesn't like fillers', or 'He won't do doubles', or 'He can't do stiles'. The emphasis is always on what the horse will or will not do, but the rider must recognize that perhaps she has changed her style when approaching the bogey fences, immediately alerting the horse and making him suspicious.

Of course a young horse is going to peek at anything he considers a little spooky, but he will either gain or lose confidence from the way the rider lets this inexperience affect her riding. A naughty horse will be well on the lookout for any change that might give him an excuse to play up, so do not give it to him!

You must look for a consistency of impulsion on all the approaches to every sort of jump, and drill yourself into not

1

changing the rules just at take-off point. Even the silliest horse will gradually discover that he need not stop: it will be much nicer for him to be co-operative than to put up with all the resulting unpleasantness and ill humour from his rider. The correct way to become consistent with the presentation is by using gridwork.

The Naughty Horse: Rescholing for Obedience and Co-operation

A horse that is an habitual stopper, refusing and napping at everything, must go right back to the beginning. Treat him like a complete novice, and build your grid as prescribed earlier, starting with poles on the ground. Use only plain poles. It will be helpful if you can place the grid next to a wall or fence, as you will only need to prevent him running out in one direction. If this is possible, it is essential to tackle the grid from both directions until he is going equally well both ways. If there is no wall, be prepared to use sloping poles as extra wings to encourage a straight approach, and make sure you keep changing the rein.

Just because you are sure the horse has the capability to jump bigger fences, do not be tempted to skip any of the stages. Be very firm in your attitude, especially as the grid increases in size, but do try to keep your approach consistent. Looking up is very important: the instant you let your eyes be drawn to the poles, there will be a corresponding giving of the contact, resulting in an immediate loss of impulsion. However hard you try not to give away the contact, it is an instinctive reaction to 'go' to the jump, and this can

only be overcome with a great deal of repetitive practice.

Be positive

As soon as you get in front of the horse, both mentally and physically, you will be unable to produce the correct degree of strength of leg into your contact and he will stop.

Building up the grid gradually and being very positive in your attitude will give him no excuse to stop. Remember, the jumps should be small enough for him to be able to step over from a standstill if necessary, and you must not let him choose to turn away. If he does stop, either make him step over, or dismantle the jump until it is small enough to do so. Turning is not to be an option: he must accept that he is to go forward, even against his wishes.

With perseverance and persistence, the horse should soon be going over your three-in-a-row grid without too much trouble, as long as you keep nagging away with your leg. Do not forget to approach on either rein, and just be alert to any hint of him hanging one way or losing a sense of rhythm. Correct any such tendency with more leg, remembering particularly to use the outside leg to kick him away from a favoured corner. If you can anticipate where he is going to hang, use the outside leg or even a tap with your stick into, past, and out of the preferred area.

Make sure the distances are fairly short, around 5.8–6.7m (19–22ft) for a 16hh horse, and as little as 5.25–5.5m (17–18ft) for a smaller animal. He does not need an excuse to stop, so you do not want him pretending he cannot reach the second and third fences just because you have given him too far to stretch himself.

Overcoming the stopping habit

When your horse is resigned to popping through this small grid, only about 45cm (18in) high, you can start to practise overcoming his stopping habit.

Riding correctly with lots of impulsion has made it easier for your horse to go rather than stop, and has been a good exercise to practise for his consistency. The jumps are sensibly small, well within his scope to pop over very easily, and you have been patient in producing him to be obedient. You are quite happy and confident and feeling the horse coming nicely up underneath you. So how will you cope when he says 'No!'?

If he is silly and/or naughty, he will say 'No' the moment you ask him to do something different. This is where you use the sheer repetitive nature of your gridwork to help you sort out his problems. Working over plain poles and gradually increasing the size has not given him anything to spook at, or any reason to be difficult. In order to produce him consistently over any sort of obstacle, you must learn how to ride him when he suddenly switches off and says 'Enough!'

Remove the first placing pole, and change it to the brightest coloured pole you can find (Fig 12). This will make him very reluctant to jump into the grid, and he will try to refuse the first jump.

Approach in trot. You will need more leg to overcome his reluctance to go forward when he sees the new pole. Think more leg but no faster – the simplest method of producing more impulsion – and try not to look down at it yourself. All your previous work has been geared up to your not looking directly at the jump. You must feel what is happening underneath you, not peek to see, and as soon as you feel the horse

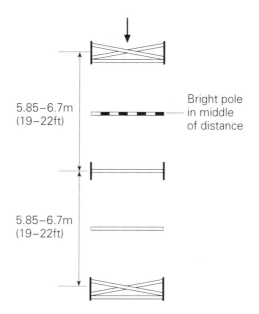

5.85–6.7m (19–22ft)

Bright pole in middle of distance

5.85–6.7m (19–22ft)

Horizontal poles 45–60cm (1½ –2ft) high
Parallel spread 60cm (2ft) maximum

Fig 12 The stopper grid.

spook, maintain your body position and contact and kick him up into your hand. Do not ride the jump. Ride the *horse*, so that he is in a position to do the jump for you. If all your attention is focused on the fence, you will incline towards it yourself and lose all the impulsion you have been working so hard to achieve.

Feel what the horse is doing. If you let him back away from underneath you, however it happens, you will not be able to get him over. If he is very spooky, approach your grid in almost a lean-back position. The second he backs off and drops the contact, it will shift you forward, and he will be able to choose for himself what to do, so make sure you do not let it happen.

Keep your weight as deep as possible into your stirrups, look up, and try to stay in that 'up' position, whatever is happening directly underneath you. You are really trying to overcome whatever tendency he has to change his rhythm and lose his impulsion. Once he has started to back off, he will be in a physical position where he will find it too difficult to do as you ask.

Be positive, mentally and physically. If he is a naughty horse, he will be pleased with the excuse to play up. Do not let him. The jumps are no more difficult, and you have only changed the appearance of them. If he refuses, you know what to do. Dismantle the first jump and kick. If you are determined to overcome his refusals, this is the way to start.

It is a shame to encourage a bout of silliness, especially if he has started to work well, but you need to be in a controlled situation to learn the most effective method for starting to deal with his problem. Inducing his willingness to stop when schooling will give you the opportunity to deal with it when there is no extra pressure to worry about. It is almost impossible to overcome a deep-rooted habit of stopping or napping when at a show, so get your horse into the habit of going at home, even against his better judgement.

The first argument will obviously be the worst, as he tries to impose his will on you, but you *know* he can go over a pole on the ground and is choosing to refuse only because he wishes to. Take particular care to ride him consistently. If he genuinely has a physical reason to stop because you have not produced enough impulsion, the whole object of the exercise is lost. However long it takes, ride him through the grid.

You *must* have a helper, ready to dismantle the poles down to the ground if necessary. If you have to keep getting on and off, the horse will have every opportunity to turn way from the grid and get his own way. An instructor would obviously be the first choice, but anyone who can move the poles is better than trying to do it alone.

You must prevail in sending the horse over the grid, even a dismantled one. Once he has accepted that he must go over the bright pole, you can gradually rebuild the grid to its original form.

When he is in a completely co-operative state and not spooking at the new pole, move it. Replace another pole with the coloured one. It does not matter if it is the second placing pole or one of the poles forming a small jump. Wherever you put it, he will notice, and if he is being naughty, again it will give you the opportunity of riding through his resistance in the most effective way.

As soon as he is used to the pole's new position and is jumping smoothly through the grid, move it again; then continue to repeat this exercise until he no longer uses the odd pole as an excuse to nap.

Crafty horses – and how to overcome them

Naughty horses have learned that however well they are ridden, they can sometimes play up in the ring with no penalty. They have discovered that the rider is more or less helpless to correct them when they only have three chances of presentation to the offending fence. Even when impeccably ridden with plenty of impulsion, if they are inclined to nap, whether caused or allowed by the current rider or a previous one, they will still try to please themselves.

The only way to cure this napping is by practising at home, and if the horse behaves perfectly well on his own home ground, substituting an unusual pole in his familiar grid is an easy way of engineering a bout of bad behaviour.

Then you can take all the time and trouble required to sort him out firmly without the additional pressure of a formal show situation. Until the horse is consenting to go through this very conventional three-jump grid without showing resistance, you have no chance of making him behave elsewhere.

Wherever the odd pole is placed, he must be ridden to accept it as normal. As long as he remains naughty, the grid will provide you with every opportunity to practise riding through any sort of nap or refusal.

Patience is absolutely essential to get the most benefit from this work. Do not hurry or bully him through the grid, even if he is being very naughty. Only a calm attitude will make him learn to cooperate in future. He needs to discover that you will not give up, even if it means dropping everything to ground level. And if he deserves a smack, this is when to do it.

When to use the stick

If the horse refuses to go into the grid because he does not like the new look of it, and you are 100 per cent certain that there is nothing physically wrong with him, *make* him do it. Use your legs and voice and keep him facing the grid, even if you have had to reduce it to ground poles. If he backs away or tries to turn, that is when he needs the stick, and if he needs a smack, do it quickly and coolly, with no accompanying loss of temper.

It is most inadvisable to smack the horse to make him jump. Reserve the use of the stick to correct him napping away from the fence, either sideways or backwards; if you get into the habit of slapping him to make him get airborne, you will always have to do it, and he will always be on the lookout to evade you.

However long you stand at the grid, keep asking him with your leg to go forward, and have the stick ready to correct anything else. He *will* learn to be obedient, as long as you approach the problem sensibly without getting at all agitated. Unless you are determined to be successful in insisting that he does what you want, you may as well give up at the beginning. The horse will always know that he can get his own way, and he will not be a pleasure to deal with.

Discipline is essential

Normally, once you have won this little battle and actually got him into the grid, the actual placement of the poles will encourage him to keep going forward. Even if you go in with a reluctant walk over the first part, consistent nagging usually produces far more willingness as he gets over the middle and last element. You will find that he will pop out over the last jump quite cheerfully, probably with relief, and will be far more willing to do it the next time round.

Once he accepts the discipline of the grid, you will both find it simpler to jump without refusing. If you make it easier for him to jump than to refuse, it will gradually sink in that obedience is preferable to napping. As long as you approach with impulsion, and the first jump remains fairly small, you will be able to increase the distance between the jumps as well as the size. Aim to increase the distance between the jumps gradually to reach 6.7–7.45m (22–24ft), remembering to move the placing poles too so that they are still in the middle of the stride.

Problem fences

If there is a particular fence that you seem to have more trouble with than

Because Teresa has built up Cyril's confidence by gradually increasing the size of the last jump on the grid, he finds it easy.

others, you may now start to introduce it as the last element in the grid. At least you will know that your striding is fine and you will not be messing up the approach by confusing your horse with your own ideas about the take-off point. This will be exactly where you need it and expect it, and both you and your horse will have gained confidence from neither stretching to the jump nor being uncomfortably close.

Many riders find spread obstacles more daunting than uprights, even if the horse is perfectly capable of coping with them. If the horse is remotely naughty, he will immediately detect a lack of rider confidence and prepare to get up to his old tricks. Build up your own confidence by gradually increasing the spread of the last jump on the grid. You should

already be popping over a small cross and horizontal jump about 60cm (2ft) wide, so change it into a very small ascending parallel.

A novice horse could be expected to spook at the change in appearance, and your naughty horse will be only too eager to notice the change too. Do not let him use it as an excuse to play up again. Think more leg but no faster on the approach. After riding through his initial resistance to the bright pole, he should then give way fairly rapidly to your determined attitude.

Depending on the capability of both horse and rider, gradually increase the height and spread of the jump. If you feel the horse is having to stretch, reduce the distance to the last fence slightly. If you feel he is getting a little close, give him a bit more room. Do not be too inflexible and try to catch him out deliberately with an awkward distance. You are looking to achieve the size of stride you hope for with no problems, so make it comfortable for the horse to do what you want. Give him his optimum take-off point for the jump that *you* do not like.

A naughty horse who has started to learn to be more co-operative will soon refuse again if *you* let him by presenting him badly to the jump. The last jump in the grid will give you the chance to establish exactly the correct degree of rhythm and impulsion over the two earlier fences. Ignore the appearance of the jump yourself by concentrating on looking away and feeling what the horse is doing. If you peek at the last jump because you do not really like the look of it, he will too.

Make the grid work for you both by gradually increasing the dimensions of the jump. The horse will hardly notice an increase in size as long as he is flowing consistently through the grid, and you should hardly feel an increase in his effort if you continue to ride the non-jumping strides in the same positive manner each time.

Once your horse has maximum impulsion, you cannot get any more. So you really must not try to wriggle about or exaggerate your position as the jumps get bigger. He is the one that needs to do more, not you. If you really feel you must try to give him some extra help, then you have not got enough impulsion. More leg and no faster will put things right. Your body movement and contact must not alter at all, or you will lose impulsion, not produce more.

Confidence from consistency
Do not give yourself too much pressure

to jump big fences immediately the horse begins to go without refusing, as you will lose any benefit acquired by your earlier patience and determination. If you build up the last jump very gradually, neither of you should be aware of it being more difficult.

Do not do too much! It is most unwise to try to be too ambitious when the horse is starting to get tired. Hopefully, your next session will be smoother and you will go through the earlier stages more quickly and conserve your energy for later on over the bigger fences.

You must go through all the stages of the grid with absolutely no hesitations or napping. Substituting the bright pole should produce no surprises. Only then will you be ready to effect the next stage of his cure.

He may take several sessions to reach this point. Do not worry and do *not* hurry. However long it takes, working your horse with a view to making him co-operative will only be doing good.

More co-operation and change
Leave the first two fences and the placing pole fairly small. Move the last jump out to form a two-stride distance, around 9.75–10.45m (32–34ft). Use two placing poles set at 3.35m (11ft) and 6.7m (22ft) from the middle jump to help you establish a good rhythm into the last fence.

These distances are suitable for a 16hh-plus horse, so reduce the distances slightly if your horse is smaller. Never forget, though, that the distances set at a show will be the same for a range of sizes from 14.3hh to 17hh plus. Eventually you will have to work with a view to producing a conventional 3.35–3.7m (11–12ft) stride, but not yet. First of all, you will need to get the horse jumping

Note how Araz's work through the grid produces the maximum impulsion from Alfie's hind leg. He finds the larger spread at the end very easy to pop over.

consistently, and if shortening the distance helps you both, do it!

Approach your grid with plenty of impulsion but not too much pace. If your previous work has been consistently produced, you should sail through the grid with no problem. If he is naughty and resistant because you are asking him to do something different, retreat a stage, drop the poles again, and remind him that his only option is to go forward.

Do make sure that you do not get anxious about the different grid yourself. The main thing to remember is that you need to give your horse consistency of directions. If your leg is always encouraging him into your hand, he should not think about hesitating. Your earlier work on the grid will already have established his co-operation, and if it has not, you must go back a stage until he becomes and remains obedient.

Good behaviour through persistence
It is not so easy to get the horse into the habit of behaving himself. If he has established that it is more fun or easier for him to refuse, he will remember this habit, and any lapses from the rider will result in his being naughty again. Try to establish consistency in your instructions, and do not be afraid to back up your wishes with your voice. He will know the difference between a growled 'bad boy' and a relaxed 'good chap'.

Initially, it will be very difficult to promote good habits in a horse who has discovered how to be naughty. The sheer repetition and disciplined approach to the grid should help, but you must be patient and persistent in keeping it up. It will work eventually: the time element depends on your determination and how long the horse has been able to please only himself.

3

4

This page and overleaf: Belinda wants Harry to practise triple bars. The grid helps her produce plenty of impulsion, and she is able to stay in balance and not allow him to lug her to the fence. To produce enough activity from the hind leg, she works hard to maintain a consistently supportive contact all the way through, trying to keep Harry in a nice co-operative outline.

Do not forget to measure the distance to the triple bar carefully and keep it a little shorter than normal. The horse must be encouraged to get in quite deep to the front rail.

5

6

7

Change again

Now your horse is popping down the grid with two strides to the last jump, make the distance into three strides: 13.5–14.75m (44–48ft) should be right, but if your horse needs a shorter distance to do three strides comfortably, do not hesitate to reduce it. Use another placing pole to encourage his stride to be even, and you should find that opening up the distance will then be very straightforward. If you do meet with resistance, deal with it in a calm manner. Reduce the size of the jumps until you can make him go over from a standstill without turning away.

You might find that as the distance is increased and the horse has more space, the approach could become crooked. He might try to take the opportunity to start to look for a way out. Obviously if you are working against a fence, this will help you stay straight and you will only have to be on guard for one side, but if you

are in the middle of the field be instantly aware of any tendency, however slight, to hang to one side or the other. Refusals are bad enough: you do not want to be coping with runouts as well. If this feels as if it might become a problem, use poles to form extra wings.

Consistent approach for obedience

If you have built up to this stage with no particular difficulty, all should be well. If it is not, just retreat a stage and re-establish the horse's willingness to be obedient. *Your* only problem would be if you allowed the change in the grid to affect your riding adversely. The extra distance could encourage you to change your style and start to urge the horse with your body and hands instead of your legs.

In the case where you only have one stride between fences, it is much easier to be consistent and not lose concentration. Three strides gives you just a little more time and room to get it wrong. Because you need to be more positive with the steering, you might forget to feel what is happening underneath you, and you might look down to the last fence instead of up and beyond it. Whatever the reason, you could get into a position where the horse does not have enough impulsion to cope easily with what you want him to do. He will become confused by your loss of consistency and revert to stopping again.

You must try very hard not to alter your riding when the grid changes. It would be such a nuisance to lose the advantage established by the earlier stages of producing the correct amount of impulsion. Do not forget why you are altering the grid. It is because your horse has a tendency to refuse, whatever the original cause, and you are trying to cure it. Changing the grid, however slightly, gives him a fresh chance to say 'No', and you a fresh chance to practise the skills that say 'Go'.

Do not throw away all the benefit of your earlier work by forgetting how to ride the in-between strides. The placing poles are a great help in establishing the rhythm and length of his stride, but you will soon need to do without them. Familiarize yourself with the nice up-tempo, regular and balanced stride that the poles are producing, because when they are removed the canter should be ridden to produce that same feeling.

Feeling right

The most difficult part of establishing the correct balance between leg and hand on the non-jumping strides in the grid is in maintaining that *feel*. It will be essential to capture that same feeling when you ask him to come off the security of the grid to try something different.

It is vital not to alter anything on the approach as the jumps change. Only when the horse is completely willing to jump the last fence from a nice balanced stride can you progress. If there is even a hint of resistance, or you feel he is finding it hard work, leave the next stage for another day.

Gradual change

Take away the placing poles, removing them one at a time, and starting with the pole nearest the second part of the grid. If your landing stride is not all it should be, you still have two poles left to help you re-establish a good rhythm into the last jump. Take it gently. There is a certain security for both you and the horse in the placing of these poles, and their removal must be carried out sensibly so that there is no loss of confidence. Because the first two elements of the grid have remained unchanged, you should be fairly relaxed with them, so then remove the placing pole between them.

Play with the grid. Change the distance to the last fence back to two strides, pull it out to 17.25–18.45m (56–60ft) for four strides. Give the horse some variety and see what he does with it. Keep the first two fences small to give you the opportunity to establish a good jumping rhythm before you tackle the bigger jump.

Do not make the distance awkward. You already know what distance suits his stride best, so stick with it. Any surprises must come from the jumps themselves, not a badly engineered spacing. You have only just got him going properly, so the last thing you need is to confuse him again by making him stretch or pop in an unbalanced, short stride.

Do not relax! It is hard work, and this

is where his old habit might surface again. You know he can be naughty: however well he is going, he is only behaving because you are giving him impulsion and making it easier for him to perform than refuse. Make the repetition of the grid help you to improve the consistency of this impulsion.

Once you are in, balance immediately so that you are in an 'up' position and able to use your leg into contact on the first stride after the jump. Then when you replace a plain pole with a bright one, you will be sharp enough to ride him forward without allowing him to hesitate as he spots it. Keep that bright pole ready and pop it in and out of the grid at random. It is a very effective way of making sure you are both quite alert. The more you practise regaining your effective position, the easier it will then be to balance up immediately after the jump. The horse must not be given a split second when he thinks he might be able to choose how to behave, because he will always make the wrong choice!

You should have done enough of this repetitive work to be able to detect any hint of bad behaviour almost before it starts, so do not slack off yourself. Keep riding the horse into your hand, and do not let him start to be lazy on the longer distance of the non-jumping strides. You know the distance will be fair for your horse. After all, you have done it so many times that you should be starting to get a feel for whether he is working correctly or not. He will not do it without your help.

Repeating the exercise over different distances should help you acquire the habit of riding every stride for 100 per cent impulsion. The horse will give up and refuse if you have made the effort of jumping too difficult for him. If you allow him to be sloppy and lazy about going forward, you will be half a stride wrong to the last jump, and will be actively encouraging him to make the wrong choice. After all, why should he put himself out and make a huge effort just because you have been inadequate?

★ You *know* that if you land and ride an up-tempo working canter you will meet the bigger jump on a good take-off point.
★ You *know* that if you do not produce this impulsion in his action, he will find it easier to refuse than jump.
★ You *know* that you will have to retreat several stages, maybe as far back as the beginning, to rebuild his confidence and co-operation.

Riders sometimes fail to appreciate that reschooling a naughty horse is very hard physical work. If you start to tire, finish the session as quickly as possible. It will be completely counter productive to carry on with it if you cannot give the exercise maximum effort, because if you are physically unable to produce the necessary impetus, your horse *cannot* – not will not – do it either.

Self Assessment

Are you up to reschooling the naughty horse? Are you physically strong and mentally bracing? Be very clear about your aims and capabilities. If your horse is so strong and self willed that you are easily exhausted, it is unlikely that you will be the one to improve him. If you find it unkind to develop a bracing attitude towards his misdemeanours, again, you may not be the one to cure him. However, if he is the horse for you, the gridwork will assuredly help you try to overcome your problems.

Be patient and positive. If the horse is physically a handful, do not try to go too far too quickly. If you feel you are tiring, have a breather, and determine to finish as soon as you can on a good note. Do not be too ambitious in what you build, relying rather on the repetition of the smaller exercises to drill him into behaving. You will soon learn how much physical effort you are able to sustain, so plan schooling sessions with the positive view of not letting yourself become too tired before you achieve what you want that day.

Your attitude is almost rather more important than your riding ability: an attitude problem can be a real hindrance to overcoming the nuisance of your horse refusing. Unless you are very determined, he will sense that you do not really want to be unkind enough to correct him. Your only option is to get tough enough over the very smallest of grids – after all, you *know* that he is perfectly capable of doing them – and then retain that attitude towards him as you very gradually increase the size of the jumps. If you are limited either physically or by a reluctance to assert yourself, it will take you some time to overcome the horse's resistance. A combination of physical fitness and a robust mental approach will give you success more quickly.

Be the boss, quite determined to be in charge. Producing and maintaining impulsion is your main aim, and you must have that in some degree to even hack up the lane. If you let the horse choose, one day he will choose to stay at home, and you will not be able to do anything at all. Naughty behaviour is always progressive, so do be positive. He will be a much nicer horse in every aspect, not only in his jumping. You do not have to face a jump to make yourself ride him properly.

Encourage your horse to give up refusing by producing enough impulsion for him to do the job more easily than not. Jumping the jumps is his business; building grids to benefit his stride, and producing impulsion so that the stride can remain active, is your department. Stay in balance into, over and away from the fence, and back up your wishes with consistency, both physically and mentally. Give the horse these advantages and, however naughty he has been originally, you *will* achieve an improvement. This may not happen immediately, but it *will* work if you persist.

SIX

Continuing the Cure

The naughty horse is learning to behave. You are sending him down a plain sort of grid without placing poles, and getting no resistance. Although he notices the substitution of a different pole, it does not cause him to hesitate. Because you are becoming sharper with your leg and more consistent with your contact, he is growing accustomed to being more amenable to your instructions.

Why shouldn't he? You are giving him all the confidence with your grid to make it easy for him to do what you want. The bigger jump no longer makes you so anxious. Your confidence in the horse and your ability to produce him has been built up gradually, and you are starting to trust each other. He is appreciating that what you want him to do will be easy, and you are beginning to recognize

Everything is fine as Paula and Zoe pop this inviting parallel in good style.

that he will not refuse if you keep giving the right instructions. You know you are going to meet the last jump at the most beneficial take-off point as long as you keep riding a good rhythm, and you are consistently managing to do so. It is ages since he tried to stop. So are you ready to try a small course away from the grid? Not yet!

Moving on – Using Placing Poles

So far, you have been working with a view to arriving at the bigger fence with the help of perfect distancing and an already established rhythm. Now you must switch your attention to the first two fences. They have remained very small throughout the exercises, and so far have been approached in trot. It is time to try the canter!

Make the first fence of the grid into a very small ascending parallel, one stride (6.7–7.45m/22–24ft) to an upright, and one stride again to a similar-sized parallel. About 60cm (2ft) high and wide would be fine to start with, but smaller of course if *you* do not like the look of it. You must not put yourself under too much pressure so that you start to feel anxious. Your horse will immediately detect your lack of confidence and wonder what has gone wrong. Do not forget, this is still a naughty horse, however nicely he has just started to perform. You cannot afford to give him the remotest opportunity to play up, whatever the cause, and whether he is bad or just cheeky, the result will be the same: refusals!

Give yourself and the horse the added security of placing poles. You will be approaching in canter, so establish a good rhythm before the first jump. If you are still pushing and accelerating to the grid, your horse will find it impossible to concentrate. You will only be distracting him from the object of the exercise, which is to make it easy for him to jump. If you allow yourself to get into a position where you are not actually holding him into the fence, you will not have impulsion. Establish that impulsion to enable your contact to be productive. If you have not got enough impetus from at least three strides away, he will find it difficult to be obedient.

The canter poles will also help if your horse starts rushing to the first jump. Beware – he might not be as enthusiastic as you think. A naughty horse can use extra pace to get the better of you; if he is dictating the speed, he will think that he can dictate everything else as well and will start up his old tricks again.

Use two placing poles set two strides (9.75–10.45m/32–34ft) and three strides (13.5–14.75m/44–48ft) from the first jump. However you approach the grid, the two poles should produce a nice balanced canter. Too fast, and they will steady you. Too slow, or lacking impulsion, and the poles will round up the stride to make it more active. Just right, and the feeling over the poles will reinforce your knowledge that you are going well.

Try very hard to maintain that rhythm into the first fence. Once you are in the grid, remember how important it is to ride the non-jumping strides properly. Do not simply sit there and be a passenger. Your horse needs the encouragement that impulsion will give him.

Increase the size of the first fence only when you feel ready. Going in over a bigger fence may cause a loss of balance on landing, and you might not be quickly enough back into position to

make the non-jumping stride quite so effective. If the horse arrives at the second fence without enough impulsion, he will find it too difficult.

Your earlier work should have given you the expertise to balance and ride your non-jumping stride. If you are being pitched forward over his shoulder, try to correct this by concentrating on landing with your weight well into the stirrup. Let your knee be as soft and flexible as possible to act as an effective shock absorber.

If you cannot absorb the extra lift and landing that a slightly bigger fence is giving, reduce the size again. Build the first jump up very gradually, so that you practise feeling your balance as you ask more. The canter poles should place you at an ideal take-off point, so you should be able to judge his movement without too much difficulty. Repeat and practise: this is the only way to improve this aspect of your riding. However much you get the theory in perspective, you have still to transfer it to your seat and saddle. You will not improve your ability much by discussing your problem, so keep repeating the exercise until you feel right about it.

When you are entirely happy with the way your horse is going through the grid, raise the middle upright. Again, your balance must be just so to enable you not only to ride the first non-jumping stride accurately, but to stay in balance again after a more steeply landed second element. Raise the middle jump very gradually so that you learn to adjust to the horse's extra effort as you go along. If you continue to pitch over his shoulder when you land, he will very soon be justified in refusing the next jump. He will have neither impulsion nor direction. Looking up as you

Opposite: However, the next fence shows that they had not quite sorted out all their problems and were not quite ready to perform without any mishap.

A stile is never popular with riders. Paula has looked down at it, tipped forward, and dropped her contact on take-off, so losing all impulsion – a perfect formula for refusals . . . and Zoe has not taken off! Prescription: a little more gridwork.

rebalance on landing will help set your weight in the right place: down into the stirrups. Looking down will only help you collapse more, as your head will already be drooping.

If you are really finding the new adjustment to a bigger grid difficult, put the placing poles in the middle of the non-jumping strides again. Until you improve, the poles will help your horse produce a nice 'up' canter stride and generate more impulsion for the second and third jump.

On Again – Removing the Placing Poles

Practise this exercise until it feels right, and then, when your confidence allows, remove all the placing poles.

So far, your horse has had a very kind introduction to the gridwork. The jumps have been small enough to approach without your panicking about the take-off point. Right or wrong on the take-off, the first two fences have been very kind, and he has not had to extend himself to do them easily. When the last jump was increased, you had confidence in the knowledge that the grid would put him in the right place to cope with something much bigger.

Now you will be unaided. Reduce the size of the first jump so that you feel entirely happy with the look of it. If you think it looks imposing, your horse will be only too willing to think so as well. Establish a good working canter, the sort of feel that the placing poles were producing. Your leg needs to be very consistent as you ride him positively into your contact. Turn to the grid only when your rhythm is established. You do not have to be in a hurry, so resist the urge to increase the pace.

Confidence

Have confidence. You would not be trying this unless the earlier work had gone well. Support your horse into the grid, do not chase him at all. Ignore completely where you think he should take off. Give him impulsion, and do not anticipate what he is going to do. Let him choose to jump from wherever he is happy. Long, short, or just so – it is not important. Stay in balance and resist the urge to organize him with your hands. If you feel you have simply got to do more, do it with the leg – and no faster!

The first jump is well within the horse's scope, wherever he chooses to jump from, and if you ensure you give him maximum impulsion, he will not make the wrong choice. And at this stage, it has got to be his choice – if you try to place him you will lose your rhythm, interfere with his concentration, and give him every opportunity to be naughty and refuse. You have done all the preparatory work to get him into the habit of going willingly, but it will not take any more than a couple of bad approaches to start him being naughty again. Logically, why should he behave consistently well if his rider is suddenly going to change the rules just in front of the jump? It is exactly where he needs distracting least.

Placing or organizing the take-off point

Obviously if you were trying to jump a 1.53m (5ft) parallel, it would be far better always to have the horse at the correct point of take-off. A more experienced rider would be able to place the horse within centimetres (inches) on his approach, and you would not see them at odds on the very last two or three strides, either.

But you are not trying to do this. You are asking your horse to jump into a small, familiar grid that he will find very easy to negotiate from almost any position as long as he has impulsion. Look where you want to go, not at what the horse is doing. All your gridwork to this point has been directed at preventing your horse from refusing, and you would not have graduated to this particular exercise if you had still been having trouble at the earlier stages, so give him impulsion and let him do it for you.

Of course, he will sometimes jump in off a long stride. Occasionally he will pop a short one in if he thinks he cannot stretch. As long as you maintain the impulsion, he will not stop, but if you try to organize anything different from the correct degree of leg to contact, he will always refuse.

Most horses will be quite happy to pop around 0.92–1.07m (3–3ft 6in) without any help at all with the take-off point. As long as they are not distracted by the rider, they will be able to make a good job of it.

Assessment and Pitfalls

It will help your overall picture of the progress you are making if you can assess accurately the current level of your horse's talent. Be aware of his capabilities and make sure you are not overfacing him. The gradual increase in size of the jumps will show you how scopey he is by the way he tackles them. Just do not make the jumps too big at the end of a long session where tiredness might contribute to a complete lack of co-operation.

There are so many pitfalls to watch out for with this sort of work, and it is very physically demanding. Horses that are hunting all day can sometimes find half an hour of this type of concentrated work enough, so keep an eye on his breathing, and give him plenty of time to recover between exercises.

Repeat this exercise until you feel blasé about your approach and are very confident about maintaining your rhythm and balance. The jumps do not have to be big, but you do need a slight increase in the size of the first two fences to encourage the horse to sort out his own strides and learn to rely on you just for impulsion.

Producing the Canter

You will be cantering in the ring, so it is just as well to start practising holding your canter at home. Make sure you do *produce* the canter: a casual approach will not do. With the earlier grid for your naughty horse, a trot approach was preferable to effect a cure. In trot, you had to keep a more consistent contact – the rhythm of the trot demanded it. In canter, it is so easy to get into the rhythm that encourages you to give your contact away. Be warned: the canter *must* be full of impulsion.

In trot, even if you had looked down, it would have been far more difficult to see where you thought the horse was going to take off, so it was easier to look away, and you were less inclined to drop your hands and lose impulsion. Once you were in the grid, the placing poles at a correct distance and a good rhythm kept your non-jumping canter strides active. However, when you approach the first jump in canter, looking down makes you anticipate take-off, with a corresponding throwing of the contact, and your horse will be encouraged to refuse.

Only when you have prepared the horse very carefully with your earlier work should you ask him to canter the first jump. The use of the placing poles will help him out initially by encouraging a nice active pace. The whole point of drilling him over this grid is to bring him willingly to the point where he canters over a combination of three fences from whatever stride and finds it easy – and does not refuse.

Do not make the grid too testing in size. It is relatively unimportant at the moment. Big jumps are not what you are hoping to achieve until later on, if at all. Remember what you began with: a naughty, napping horse that really did not want to behave or jump. Now he should go forward without question as long as he has impulsion. You want a partnership with you each helping the other. You give him impulsion. He does the job.

Setbacks

If there are any setbacks, just retreat a stage or two on the grid to re-establish your total confidence in each other. Discovering how to produce enough impulsion to prevent the horse refusing does take time, and you should never become impatient. Do not try to hurry through the earlier stages just because the jumps are small. He must do them properly, even though he may well be capable of doing much more. Sort out his problem over jumps you know cannot possibly be overfacing him. You will be far more confident, as will he.

Different Jumps

The tricky bit comes when you move away from the grid and start trying to

4

5

jump different types of jump. However, if you can brainwash yourself into riding different fences with the same feeling that you produced into the grid, the horse will be fine. Why should he stop? There will be no reason, unless the new jump is too big for him or you. Do not let that happen. Think of all the hard work you have had to do to get him jumping without refusing: how foolish it would be to throw it all away by overfacing both of you.

Think impulsion and concentrate on producing it. Never mind the jump, as long as it is not too big. Give the horse the impulsion you have learned to acquire on the grid. Naughty refusals should be a thing of the past. Just as he had got into the habit of refusing and pleasing himself, your gridwork will have imposed a certain discipline on you both. He should now have acquired the *good* habit, and as long as you make his jumping easy for him, there will be no

Opposite and left: Paula works Zoe through a grid with placing poles, substituting a double cross in the middle for a plain upright. The double cross has been used with the express intention of causing Zoe to peek and nap, giving Paula the chance to practise riding with the correct balance of leg to contact. Once Paula has got the right feeling through the grid, she must reproduce this consistently all the way round a course.

3

reason for him to lose it and revert to being naughty again.

Renewed naughtiness

What happens if you are not as successful away from the grid as you should be, and your horse starts to refuse again?

Ask yourself why this is happening. Perhaps you have rather hurried through the exercises and not given your horse time to establish and absorb this new improved behaviour. Things will only go well if you have been methodical with the earlier stages.

Once you start doing bigger grids from canter, you need several sessions with no mishaps. Make your horse really confident in your ability to give him clear instructions plus the necessary impulsion. He has been naughty in the past, whatever and whoever caused it, and he will remember what good fun it is

to get his own way again. You must be watchful to ensure that old habits do not try to re-assert themselves.

Once he has started to go well, do not rush taking him to shows. There should be no time element involved. If he is not 100 per cent at home for several schooling sessions, he will be unlikely to concentrate at a show. You will not be at your best either, unless you have the total confidence of knowing he has not stopped for a long time.

It is so easy to relax when the horse jumps nicely. Remember that he is only going nicely because you have brought him to such a condition by riding him correctly, *all* the time. If you relax, so will he, and you will both stop working.

If your horse has been 100 per cent co-operative on the grid through four or five sessions, you should be fine to try something else. But what if he still refuses at a new jump? If you are sure

Opposite and above: After several pleasing gridwork sessions, next time out is 100 per cent successful. Paula produces impulsion – Zoe produces the jump!

you have not rushed things, then you must be brutally frank with yourself.

Examine your approach honestly. Have you changed your style because you are asking him to do something fresh? Have you become apprehensive because you do not trust him to behave? Your horse will immediately sense any change in you and become suspicious. Unless you can produce him consistently in the correct manner he has become used to, he will revert to his former naughty ways.

Do not give yourself a hard time with the fresh jumps. Keep them small enough so that you do not feel your eyes drawn down to them. Your horse will be on the lookout for a change in attitude, so do not be wimpish. If you really feel you cannot approach something new without feeling anxious, go back to the security of the grid and practise the familiar exercises until you acquire much more confidence.

There is no time element. Take as long as you feel you need. Throwing away all the solid work you have done to cure his refusing is unnecessary. Wait until you are sure that a fresh jump presents no particular problem. Ignore the look of it on your approach. Ride him consistently into your contact, do not change the rules, and he will have no reason to misbehave.

It is only when you start to ride the jump rather than the horse that you will precipitate disaster, and if you do get it wrong and confuse him, you must take him back to the grid and re-establish confidence in each other again. It *will* work, but only if you do not let your nerves get the better of you and affect your riding.

It is very difficult to remain the same calm, confident person when you know you are approaching a jump that your horse has taken a marked dislike to in the past. Let the results of the solid gridwork you have been doing take over, and ride him with the same degree of confidence you discovered on the grid.

If you convince yourself that he is reforming, your horse will be convinced as well.

SEVEN

Careless Horses

Now that you are well on the way to solving the three-faults problem, the clear rounds should be coming thick and fast. But are they?

★ Now your horse is jumping the jumps, is he making a good job of clearing them, or is your progress round the ring notable only for the amount of timber he dislodges?

★ Why does your horse knock poles down? Do you have a mild case of 'four-faultitis', or do you leave the ring with the course looking like a battlefield?

★ Does he choose one particular type of fence to hit, or is he more versatile, tipping everything regardless?

★ Does it only happen in jump-offs?

★ Is it a tip or a real bang – back legs, front legs, or all four? Do you think he is careless or clumsy or both?

★ Do you think the course builder is unfair with his distances, so that you meet the fences badly?

★ Are you getting too close to the fence, or standing off too far away? Do you tell him off with a grumpy 'hey' or similar every time you touch a pole? If he does not understand that you do not like it, why should he try that bit harder to clear them?

★ And do you occasionally rattle a pole and admit that it might be your fault?

Whatever the reason for your horse failing to jump every fence cleanly, you should be able to do something to help him improve by using gridwork.

Occasional Taps in Front

The occasional knockdown with the front legs may be caused by a slightly casual approach. An occasional tip in the ring will happen to anybody, but you want to do something about it before it becomes a habit.

Build a fairly conventional grid: small spread to small upright on 6.7–7.45m (22–24ft) for one stride, and the same distance again to a small spread at the end. Make the grid smaller than the size you are currently competing over.

Canter in to the grid and try to analyze what is happening underneath you. If you can hear the horse tapping poles all the way through, you have a problem, and it will probably be caused by your being slightly out of balance in the air. If your horse is keen, he will be taking you forward to the grid. You will have a strongish feel from your contact, making it difficult to judge how much leg to use on the non-jumping strides. Too much leg will only make him go faster if you cannot contain the pace to produce impulsion instead of speed. If he is enthusiastic in the grid, you will then find that he is making up a little too much ground. If he gets too close to the second and third element, he will have neither time nor room to haul his front legs up out of the way cleanly.

The simplest method of producing a better-balanced effort in the air is to sharpen up your weight distribution. Put a placing pole in the first distance, but *not* in the middle of the stride. Instead, move it at least a 30cm (1ft) closer to the landing side of the first jump. Do the same on the second non-jumping stride. The pole will discourage the horse from running on and making up too much ground. He will have a bit more room in front of the jumps, and hopefully the pole will have steadied him slightly, so there will be more time and space to get up cleanly. You will be able to help as well by concentrating on the balancing of your weight. You have got to improve yourself because you will not be able to use placing poles at a show. They are only there now to help you get the right *feeling*: the feeling that you must reproduce with your leg, contact and balance.

If you land in a heap after the first jump, your weight will be too far forward over the horse's shoulder, so he will find it more difficult to lift his front end with the extra weight hanging there. Really make the effort to look up and get your weight landing deeply into the stirrups through a nice flexible giving of the knee. The softer you can relax through your knee, the easier it will be to stay in balance with your horse.

Your contact must also be more consistent. Loopy reins will positively encourage him to collapse in front, because you will be producing no impulsion to help him stay light. Result: a long, flat stride giving a lazy, flat jump.

Keep hold, and be in a position to use your leg and *ride* the non-jumping stride instead of just being a passenger. The placing poles will steady the horse a touch and give you a bit longer to get your balance right. Be determined to take full advantage of the split second longer between the fences to organize yourself. Looking up, is of course, essential, as it will help to keep your body in the 'up' position.

You must ride this non-jumping stride with the express purpose of producing impulsion. If you 'give' the hand to the jump, you will instantaneously lose your power when you need it most. Resist the urge to 'go' to the jump in front of the horse. He will only be distracted, and if he is prone to tapping an odd pole, he will have every excuse to do so.

High crosses

If your horse is very casual, you might have to do something extra to make him a bit snappier. Leave the distances and the placing poles the same, but make a high cross in the middle of the grid.

The middle of the cross will not be so high, but the optical illusion produced by the narrower sides will make him back off and take notice. Again, this will give you the chance to hold him in balance and get a little more leg on. The new appearance of the grid will make him concentrate and steady slightly. Take this opportunity to practise being that little bit quicker to land in balance, and keep hold.

You must get to know what the *feel* of contact and balance should be like to get the maximum lift from your leg, since it is your leg that is the key to all your jumping success. The contact and balance must be right to enable your leg to be effective in producing impulsion, both forward and upward.

Your horse will definitely elevate over the high cross from a more civilized and steadier stride – just make sure you have enough leg on in case he backs off a little too much! You should get a really nice rounded feel in the air, and if he then carries you out of balance to the last, make that into two high crosses forming a parallel about 60cm (2ft) wide. He will take more notice of the jump as it will look odd, giving you the chance to get more leg on into your contact. If he is still pulling you into the grid, high cross the first jump too if you like, but do not make it look quite so imposing.

Using the look of the poles is a very sensible way to go about making a horse more careful, and is infinitely preferable to building too big a fence in the hope of getting more 'lift'. Overfacing always does more harm than good, and will definitely not give the horse confidence or encourage extra effort in picking up his feet.

This exercise is purely to get you into the habit of feeling the necessary balance and strength of leg into degree of contact which is producing a cleaner jump. Playing with the poles and the high crosses will help you develop your skills. They look odd, the horse will take more notice, and he will be a little more amenable to accepting your directions. The extra time he takes between the fences, however slight, will give you more chance to be in the right place to make those directions clear. Rider errors include:

★ Collapsing over his shoulder on landing – the horse will be careless at the next jump.
★ Giving the contact a fraction on take-off – the horse will be careless.
★ Expecting speed to carry you through

instead of impulsion from your leg – the horse will be careless.

Do not make these errors.

Repeat the exercises so that you can learn how the non-jumping strides should feel and be ridden before you tackle the more conventional grid again. Do not forget your voice. Tell your horse when he is getting it wrong, even if the problem has arisen because you have given the contact or tipped forward or both. He will not know that it is your fault, and can still try to pick his feet up if he knows you prefer it.

One Careless Leg

Habitually touching the poles with one particular foreleg is extremely annoying. Most horses favour one side, and possibly his early schooling has not corrected his tendency to be lazy on one particular rein. You may also have a tendency to be one sided with your weight distribution. Whichever it is, the grid will help.

First discover if the horse is ambidextrous or is only being casual with one particular foreleg. Build a conventional grid – small parallel to upright to small parallel on 6.7–7.45m (22–24ft) distances – against the fence or wall. Jump the grid on both reins and have someone experienced watch the horse. Does he always touch the pole with his inside front leg, changing the careless leg as you change rein? Or is it the same careless leg from each direction? Alternating the careless leg has much to do with your balance and anticipation of turning, and will be the next habit to deal with.

If you are sure that he always trails the same leg, whichever rein he is on, you will be able to help prevent this. Build a grid with small bounce crosses: a double cross to three single crosses on 3.35m (11ft) and another double cross at the end. Pop him through the grid and note if he taps the poles. Growl at him. Try again.

If he still touches the poles, whichever leg is offending, raise that side of the single crosses by at least 30cm (1ft). The size of the jump will hardly increase in the middle, but will be substantially different on the side of the erring leg. Be prepared to grumble at him if he is still tapping the poles, and make it an instantaneous reaction as soon as you hear him. You do need to *tell* him that this is not acceptable. If he is cleanly picking up one foreleg, there is no reason for him not to snap up the other one. This grid will make him try a bit harder, especially if you tell him off.

If he starts to be a little more accurate in the middle but still taps the last double cross, raise the same side of the first pole as you have the small crosses, and raise the opposite side of the further cross by the same amount. It will be an odd-looking parallel, a 'St Andrew's Cross'. The pole towards him will be higher on the offending side, and the back pole will already look odd enough to encourage him to make more effort.

If you find this is starting to have an effect, praise the horse but do not alter the grid. Practise using it as it is, always remembering to scold if you hear him tap. If he remains careless, make the same sort of fence going into the grid, and use fairly substantial poles.

The grid will certainly help him get into the habit of raising both front legs equally. Use it as often as necessary, because the horse will find it quite easy to slip back into his lazy way if you allow

him. In addition, it will only effect a cure if you ride it purposefully. However much improvement you get, you will probably still have to use this grid occasionally to remind him how to pick his feet up equally.

Your approach should be bouncy and active. Use a canter pole if you are worried about your take-off point, but you must set it at least three strides (13.5–14.75m/44–48ft) away. The grid should not be big enough to make you anxious about your approach, but if the placing pole helps you, then use it.

Maintain a good contact as you approach and concentrate completely on keeping your shoulders level. Most riders favour one side and are inclined to drop their weight unequally in the stirrup; if you think 'shoulders level' your weight distribution will stay equal all the way down.

If you are completely confident that you are straight and level on your approach, make sure you get an equal feel into each stirrup as you jump. The grid will certainly help, but you have to be able to produce your horse properly to get the most improvement out of him. Concentrate on being deep down into your stirrup, but looking up and ahead in a straight line. Your horse will detect immediately if you are feeling even slightly one sided, and it will be enough to make him careless. Whichever side your weight favours, that will be the side he will tap.

Through the bounces, let your knee be soft enough to absorb the motion. Try not to allow your lower leg to escape back and up. Your sense of balance needs to be deep and secure, with your weight totally into the stirrup irons and hanging from the stirrup bars. If your weight is always hanging from the same

Opposite:
Candy usually trails her left foreleg slightly. This grid will help Lesley to correct this tendency.

point, your horse will find it much easier to adjust to you on his back. If you are constantly altering your first point of balance, either too far forward or too far back, you will always be distracting the horse from doing his job properly and making it far more difficult for him to clear the poles properly. If your weight correctly balanced, you will find it simpler to get enough leg on into your contact to produce a nice active rhythm.

As you progress down the grid, do not allow the bounces to encourage you to tip more and more forward. You must keep your weight off the horse's shoulder and hanging consistently and equally off the stirrup bars. As soon as you tip forward, and of course you know already that looking down will encourage this, your contact will go and you will have loopy reins. Your horse will lose the support from your hand, and he will not be in an active enough position to be able to 'snap up'. If he is inclined to trail one leg, this is when he will do it.

Although the structure of the grid will help you to insist that he raises the lazy leg, so much depends on your riding well enough to ensure that your unlevel weight does not cause any more unnecessary carelessness.

Hanging to One Side

This type of grid is also very helpful if your horse hangs to one side or the other. If you find it difficult to keep him straight because he drifts from your steering, try it. It should not take him long to realize that it will be easier to stay in the middle of the crosses rather than opting for the higher side, but do try to analyze why it happens in the first place.

Perhaps you bought him with this tendency, or your steering signals are

unclear. Maybe your weight distribution is one sided. Whatever the cause, this particular grid is custom built to help you solve this problem just as well as it helps improve the dangly leg, but the problem will certainly return unless you use the grid to correct your riding as well as the horse's inclination to hang.

The same advice given for the dangly leg applies for the hanging horse. Practise *riding* the grid, and decide which aspects of your riding you need to concentrate on for a better result. Even if you think it is not your fault, you have still got to solve the problem. Help the poles to help the horse by providing him with the impulsion and guidance to do the job properly.

Front Leg Rider Error

There is another cause for your horse knocking poles in front, and it is entirely the rider's fault. Very often the rider gets the horse off the ground nicely and then collapses in mid-air. This is a more common occurrence when the rider does not really like the look of the jump. Once she has done enough on the ground to produce a nice accurate take-off, she can almost relax with relief. There is a loss of balance in the air and the horse relaxes too – and is too relaxed to stay sharp in front.

Build a conventional grid: small ascending parallel to small ascending parallel on 6.7–7.45m (22–24ft) and then to a true parallel on 9.75–10.45m (32–34ft). The last jump is a true parallel on a two-stride slightly shorter distance than normal, to make the grid more difficult. If you collapse the tiniest fraction after take-off, you will hit the front pole. You will also hit the front pole if you do not ride the non-jumping stride in an 'up' position and into a consistent contact. Decide what aspect of your riding you are concentrating on improving. As long as your non-jumping strides are ridden well, you should be able to pinpoint the problem as being one of the 'good boy' syndrome.

Establish your balance and rhythm over the first two elements and make sure you ride your two-stride distance with plenty of impulsion and not too much speed. As your horse starts to come up underneath you, do not be tempted to think you have done enough. All the way over the jump, concentrate on keeping your weight well into the stirrup to produce a secure lower leg, a good solid base for your balance. If you are not in balance, you will not be able to hold the light, consistent contact necessary to keep the horse concentrating and well up over the jump.

Do not be tempted to exaggerate your seat and tip too far forward – looking up and away will certainly help to overcome this – and do not let your contact go loopy in the air. The only reason your horse is jumping nicely is because you have produced impulsion and, even in the air, you should not allow yourself to change the style. Of course, you are only being supportive with your hand, not too strong, but you should maintain a nice feel to avoid distracting him. So many riders feel that they have to 'give' over a fence, meaning they exaggerate the movement of their hands forward. They do not want to catch the horse in the mouth, and of course this attitude is entirely commendable – but it does not work. All you will produce is loss of impulsion when you need it most, and careless front legs. When you land there will be far more movement of your body to rebalance, and retaking the contact

again is a major distraction, especially in a combination. If your horse is keen, strong, or disobedient he will have every opportunity to assert himself while your reins are loopy.

When you drop your weight deep into the stirrup and allow your body to follow the horse's effort naturally, your hands will 'give' quite enough with your body motion. You do *not* need to move them independently. As long as your wrists and elbows are flexible and do not remain fixed and rigid, your body motion will be enough.

Degree of Contact

It is usually drummed into young riders from a very early age that they must give with their hands over a fence. Of course, you do not want to be hanging on by the reins and beginners should employ a neckstrap, but as practice helps the beginner's balance to develop, so she should then start to feel the necessary consistent, supportive contact. On the other hand, if your reins are held too strongly over the fence you will create worse problems: your horse will jump in a hollow outline and hit everything that is behind, and you will both find it most uncomfortable.

Try to look for the middle-of-the-road approach. Maintain the contact – a supportive feeling – and try not to change things in the air. There are one or two variations to the grid that will help you to circumvent this contact problem and encourage you to produce the right feel. Practise with these, but do remember that they are only helping you in the right direction. The grids will definitely cure the immediate problem of knocking poles at the time of the exercises, but eventually you will have to brainwash yourself into producing the same high quality of riding in the ring.

Increase the height and width of the last jump, the true parallel. Do not be too ambitious for your horse's ability, but try to make it look a little imposing to you. Put a placing pole three strides (13.5–14.75m/44 to 48ft) from the last jump on the grid. Keep the first two jumps straightforward, and concentrate on producing a nice rhythm through the grid. Your impulsion should be fine. But what about the last jump? It is going to take a bit more effort: it is the last jump in the line, and it looks more difficult. If you think 'good boy' as the horse takes off, you are halfway towards having it down in front.

Relaxing is not an option for you or the horse – you have not finished yet. You have three good strides to ride to the placing pole, and being in a position to ride those three strides is the most important part of the exercise. If you do not produce them, you will get that pole wrong as you will not have enough impulsion to reach it on three.

Think ahead if you tend to collapse over a bigger obstacle. Do not be grateful because you have taken off. If you *are* airborne, do not spoil the jump by collapsing and encouraging your horse to hit it. Think about producing a good landing stride and using it, even if it is the last jump. It will focus your attention on riding away from the fence and hopefully prevent your collapsing in the air. However pleased you are with the horse's effort, do not relax before you have finished. Be positive into, over and after the jump. If you know you have got more to do, your concentration should remain focused and you will be far less likely to hit the poles.

As with all your jumping exercises, you are looking for consistency. Do not

distract the horse by changing things. Riding down to the placing pole should ensure that you do not relax over the fence, because you know you have still not finished.

'Good boy' syndrome is an attitude problem that will spoil an otherwise foot-perfect round – and it is *your* attitude problem, not the horse's. It must be cured. When your horse takes off at a jump you really do not like the look of, you feel a surge of relief.

★ You will let that relief cause you to collapse in the air
★ You will probably knock down the jump
★ You will develop a 'thing' about that particular jump (and why is it usually planks?).

Your horse will be blameless, but you will still think it is the jump that has been the problem, not your own attitude which is causing you to collapse in the air. Analyze the cause of your knock-downs carefully to see if 'good boy' syndrome is anywhere to be detected, and own up to it. It would be such a shame to be apprehensive about a particular jump if your attitude caused the original mishap.

Other Ways of Scoring Four Faults

If a course builder is anticipating a large entry, one of his favourite methods of weeding out the competitors is to place a parallel before a fairly sharp turn. It will cause numerous knockdowns, and this is not entirely due to the actual size and appearance of the jump: the rider will anticipate the turn and distract the horse a little too early with her steering efforts. This is not quite the same cause as the 'good boy' syndrome, but has similar results, and a similar grid will help to cure the problem.

If you drop your shoulder and hint too strongly in the air about the direction in which you intend to go, your horse will drop his shoulder too and will hit the poles. Certainly you should be thinking about the direction you want to take, but you must be very subtle with timing the signals. Too soon, and he will be distracted in the air. Too late, and you will miss the turn.

If you are working at the side of a school, obviously the horse will know he has got to turn at the end, and there will not be a choice of direction either. If you allow it, he will be ready to anticipate the turning too, perhaps collapsing the inside front leg a touch early while he is still over the fence. The horse must be encouraged to land fair and square after his efforts. The signal to turn should come when he has all four legs on the ground. Later on, when you and your horse are an experienced combination, you will want to be turning in the air in jump-offs. There are grids that will help you do so cleanly, but for the moment you need to concentrate on consistently producing accurate clear rounds, so leave the ambitious turns for now.

If you allow or even actively encourage your horse to anticipate the turn after landing, he will become careless. As soon as you drop your shoulder or give away the contact with your outside rein, he will be distracted and very inclined to drop his inside front leg. He will probably land on the wrong leg in canter too, which certainly will not help him to negotiate the turn in a balanced rhythm.

Build the same grid that you used for the 'good boy' correction, and have the last fence fairly close to the end of the school. Place a canter pole round the corner, carefully measuring the correct distance to correspond with following the optimum route – this will be 17.25–18.45m (56–60ft) for four strides – and measure the route to allow for one perfectly straight stride after the grid (Fig 13).

Because the grid is near the end of the

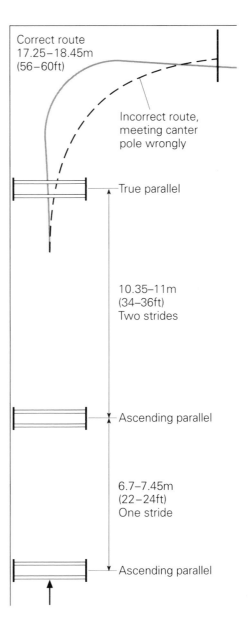

Fig 13 Ride the corner – do not become a passenger.

school, your horse will be already thinking 'turn' as he goes through it. Take a particularly positive contact with the outside hand on the two non-jumping strides to the last fence. Think straight, and do not let any anticipation creep into your riding attitude. Keep your shoulders level over the fence and ride the first non-jumping stride away from the fence in a straight line. Only then give him the signal to turn. If you take the correct route over the grid and round the corner, the canter pole should be taken perfectly in the middle of his stride. Your rhythm and balance will be established immediately to carry on nicely on the correct leg, and you should have cleared the jump easily.

If your outside aid has been too strong, your corner will be too square and you will find the distance long, but you will probably have landed in correct canter. The rhythm will be easy to re-establish, you will be in a good position to carry on round a course if necessary, and you should not have hit the jump.

If you have allowed the horse to anticipate the turn, the distance will be too short, as he will fall in round the corner from the first stride. Because your outside contact has been too light through the grid, he will anticipate turning as he takes off. If you have let him pull you over to the inside, your shoulders will be unlevel and you will not be well balanced. Because the outside rein is too kind, he will land on the wrong leg and be totally unbalanced round the turn, losing both impulsion and rhythm – and he will probably have knocked down the pole as well.

Practice the grid on both reins until you get the right feeling to ride the optimum route. Try to concentrate on producing a straight line down the whole of the grid. Be ready to use more outside rein to hold the horse straight, because he will try to lean every time. He does know which way he has got to go – the walls see to that. How you meet the placing pole will determine if you have got it right or not, and of course, if it is wrong you will hear him hit the jump.

Once your horse is being obedient, and you are not anticipating the turn yourself, move the grid to a more open space where you can turn either way at the end of it. Still use the placing pole to impose the discipline on his stride and direction, but put one for each rein.

Practise the grid turning both ways, but vary the order. Your horse will soon learn if you change rein each time, and he will start to anticipate that too. You are still looking to land on a straight stride after the last jump in order to jump it cleanly, and are still trying to steer and ride the rhythm to help you meet the placing poles accurately.

The grid will sharpen up your balance and your whole attitude. Immediately you start to become slack and anticipate the direction too early, you will collapse in the air – and so will the horse. The result will be knockdowns.

EIGHT

Careful Horses make Mistakes

Why does the careful horse get four faults? A careful horse is a joy to own, but even the most careful of animals will occasionally make mistakes. The rider will usually be to blame, but sometimes the horse itself will develop a little problem. Whoever is in the wrong, the fault must be corrected.

The Classy Novice

Horses with a lot of ability will rapidly jump out of their novice classes, and sometimes too quickly to have learned their job properly. Once they have then moved up a class, they will simply not be experienced enough to cope if their technique is undeveloped. They will not have had enough experience to teach them to fold their legs up out of the way.

These horses usually have a lot of talent and have found the early classes very easy. They have developed a style of jumping higher than strictly necessary to clear the poles: you will often find novice horses ballooning in the air and jumping far higher than the fence requires. This style shows enthusiasm but a lack of experience; they have not learned to fold their legs neatly to avoid the poles.

And what happens when the jumps get bigger? The horse cannot keep ballooning in the air and clearing the fence by the same margin.

Clearing 1.23m (4ft) in the air over a 60cm (2ft) pole is easy; jumping 1.54m (5ft) over a 92cm (3ft) pole is not. It will simply require too much effort to keep it up, and it will not be too comfortable for the rider either.

Faced with larger jumps, the horse will start to rattle poles, purely because his technique is wrong and needs improving. It will not do anything for his confidence either, if he thinks he always has to jump half a metre higher than he really needs to. The sooner the talented novice learns to snap up his legs, the easier he will find the bigger jumps.

Bounce Grids

Build a grid of small crosses at the bounce distance of 3.35–3.7m (11–12ft). Start with a double cross, have three or four single crosses in the middle, and finish with a double cross on a slightly longer distance, about 30cm (1ft) extra. Work your horse through the grid and practise establishing a rhythm. Think 'down' with your weight rather than forward and do not be in a hurry. You should be coming out of the grid with the same rhythm, contact and pace as when you go in.

If your horse is overdoing the height, do not worry. Just keep your leg on and encourage him to go forward into your consistent contact. As the crosses come a bit thick and fast, he will start to realize he need not get so high in the air. He will not really have time, because he will need to get his legs down for the next cross, and he will discover that the whole exercise will be easier for him if he does not make such a huge jumping effort.

Once the horse is going smoothly – and the distance and smallish size of the crosses should soon establish this – raise the last cross to make a horizontal pole, only about 45–60cm (1½–2ft) high. Ignore the change yourself and keep presenting the horse to the grid with the same approach: impulsion, contact, rhythm and balance. Let your weight hang consistently down from the stirrup bars so that the horse will not be distracted by any exaggerated movement from its rider.

Again, if all goes smoothly, raise the next cross to form a small true parallel out of the grid. You will then feel a bit more lift, although the slightly longer distance to this jump will help the horse to stay smooth. As long as he jumps through the grid with no problems, raise each cross in succession, working from the last to the first. When you get to the point of raising the first double cross, widen the distance out by 30cm (1ft) to give a little more room. If he sails in too boldly over the first fence he must not be penalized by finding the distance too short for comfort.

You will find this exercise invaluable in improving your contact and balance. You will know if you get it wrong, because your horse will hit the poles. The row of horizontal bounces with parallels at each end will not give the horse time to get too high or dangle his legs. If he does not snap up his legs out of the way, he stands no chance of being accurate. Remember, he is a careful

horse, and you are trying to make his technique more effective before he is asked to jump higher fences. You are trying to improve him, not to catch him out.

If he finds this grid difficult, be persistent but not stupidly unbending. If you have to reduce the size of the bounces to make him comfortable, then do so. If you need to lengthen the distances slightly to give him more room and time, do so. You are hoping to make every effort easier, not more difficult. The very positioning of the bounce poles should encourage him to fold his legs up, rather than have him thinking he has to go so high.

Build the grid up very carefully. Confidence is very important, and the grid must not be too sharp for him at this stage. The repetition of the work will help him to realize that it does not require so much lifting effort, and he will eventually get the idea of folding his legs a little more effectively. Just be very careful that the poles are not too high or the distance too short.

A *gradual* build-up on *both* reins is essential, and you must reduce the bounces to crosses again when you change rein. Do not be lazy about altering the grid. You should not expect him to change rein and immediately be proficient going the other way. Take a lot of time and trouble to build this grid correctly. After all, you are trying to help a good horse, not reschool a naughty one.

If your horse leaves the grid and immediately starts ballooning again over other jumps, repeat the bounce exercises. However bright and talented he is, it will take him a little time to learn that he does not have to go too high over the fences, and repetition of this rather difficult exercise will help him develop

The author and Spud
making a serious effort
at a show. Note how the
'Stay Clean at Speed'
grid produces a clean
pair of heels in this
winning round.

The author and Beaconsfield Majestic (Spud) schooling at home over a bigger fence after doing gridwork.

A combination obstacle is only a dressed-up grid. The value of gridwork is demonstrated in how easily the author and Spud jump through this combination of parallel to upright.

Looking up, looking away: such a good habit to get into.

A horse that hangs one-sided or has one careless front leg will benefit immensely from this type of grid. Brenda keeps Millie on a true line.

The author and Spud working through a grid specifically designed to help him jump clear in a jump-off. Note how the placing poles help to produce a rounded stride leading to accurate jumping.

Gemma makes Teazel repeat this 'Stopper' grid until Teazel takes no notice whatsoever of the different placings of the coloured pole.

Paula brings Zoe nicely out of the 'hit-and-hurry cure'. The canter poles on the way in produce an accurate approach, and, when ridden correctly, the poles out give a well-balanced exit.

Araz is determined to ride Alfie on the optimum line back down the 'every which way' grid from fence B to the bounces.

A nice line across from C to D on the square grid, with Sarah already giving subtle signals for Charlie to turn left-handed after the fence.

Plenty of impulsion, consistent light rein contacts and balanced positions: whether schooling or competing, these horses and riders all demonstrate the expertise that gridwork has produced in each partnership.

Improving jump-offs:
Mary and Charlie have
kept a good line across
from A to D and are
already preparing for
the short left turn to B.

the skills that will save him a lot of superfluous effort.

Who else will this grid benefit?

The Careless Schoolmaster

The same structure of grid will also wake up the good horse who has got a little rusty or complacent, and will remind the schoolmaster to pick his feet up all the time.

Perhaps he has been jumping courses that are a little too small for him. Schoolmasters will sometimes encounter this problem if they change riders, as the standard of competition will be downgraded to allow the fresh rider to become acclimatized to jumping fences on the older horse. Until the rider gains experience, the horse will be asked to jump much smaller courses than he has been used to, and unless the rider soon comes up to standard, he may feel lower jumps are not worth bothering with.

A schoolmaster type is usually very wise and careful. He will know exactly how much effort to put in to carry a novice rider safely round a course of jumps, and he will not maintain that effort unless the rider begins to improve. Even the most genuine and capable schoolmaster might become careless, and you need the grid to both help and encourage him to regain his attitude and proficiency.

The size of the jumps may be smaller to allow for the rider's inexperience, but keep the distances the same. The horse needs to practise as well as the rider. Even with a novice on top, the grid will sharpen up the older horse and allow him to teach the rider to develop his balance and rhythm. It will also be the quickest method of bonding a new and effective partnership.

The Good Horse

The good horse has probably been jumping well at shows. He knows about bigger jumps and more effort. If he is jumping well in the ring, he will not need to practise over big fences at home to keep him up to scratch. A few times down this type of grid will loosen him up between shows and help him remain neat and tidy in the air.

A little bit of homework before he goes out again will ensure that he stays a good horse, and this grid is exactly the sort of work that he should be doing. It is also extremely beneficial for the rider, whether novice or experienced, as the balance and contact must be immaculate.

Build the same grid as for the careful but exaggerated jumper, but keep the distances equal all the way through. If the horse has been competing, keep the distances slightly on the shorter side: 3.35m (11ft) maximum. Build up the grid gradually, jump by jump, to form the horizontal bounces. Do not make them too high to start with; about 60cm (2ft) is fine. Because you have not increased the two end distances to help him, he will need to be very careful to avoid touching the poles. Scold him if he does this.

Approach the grid in a strong, bouncy canter. You will really feel the horse coming up into your hand, so make sure that hand is keeping a consistent contact. If he goes in boldly over the parallel, he will have to snap up very sharply for the first single pole.

You must be able to feel what is happening underneath you and to then adjust your balance into the stirrups accordingly. If you get left behind or tip much too far forward, your weight will unbalance him and he will not be able to perform accurately through the series of

bounces. It will be very uncomfortable for you both. If you are wrong going in, use the knowledge of what sort of feel the grid produces to try to re-establish balance and contact after the mistake. You know what he will be doing, so try to feel enough to catch up with him if necessary, or wait for him to come up again underneath you. Deviate from the perfect position with your balance, or give too much with the contact, and he will be unable to cope with the grid.

This particular grid will really make him athletic and sharp, and should do exactly the same for you. It is just the sort of practice you both need in between shows to keep your eye in and stay jumping fit. It will, however, be extremely hard work, both for you and the horse, so do not overdo it – four or five times over the raised poles on each rein is plenty if you are doing it correctly. If you or your horse are making mistakes, leave enough time between exercises to get your breath back. It will be totally unproductive and rather foolish to try to work through this grid without being able to give it 100 per cent effort because you are far too tired or breathless.

If you cannot get it right in one session, drop the middle crosses again and work over them until you are satisfied. Leave it for another day before increasing the size again. Do *not* hurry! Rushing your grids will not make them work any better for you, so be patient.

Timing Errors

Timing is most important when you are jumping bigger fences, particularly with your balance in the air over wider parallels. This grid will help you develop accurate timing in your balance so that you can avoid getting four faults.

The distances are short and sharp. Unless you are aware of what is going on underneath you, you won't be able to adjust your weight accordingly, so you must learn to feel the timing necessary to avoid causing knockdowns.

If you are a little in front of the horse through the grid, he will not be supported with the contact. Your leg will be unable to be effective in the rhythm of the grid, and he will lack impulsion. He will also lack the supporting hand to help him snap up, so he will hit the poles in front.

If you misjudge the horse's action, you will anticipate the landing between poles. You will shift your weight to adjust for the landing a split second too early and he will hit the poles behind.

In the grid, concentrate on hanging in balance from the stirrup bars. Maintain a consistent contact so that your leg can produce impulsion all the way through. Do not get over the first jump and think you have done enough. You must help the horse all the way along and not just become a passenger. Beware of losing rhythm, because you will be totally at odds with the horse and unable to help him. All the balance required to negotiate any type of jump can be improved by working through short, sharp bounces, but the timing must be right.

Do not ask too much from either yourself or the horse. It would be very easy to build this grid to be unjumpable. If the poles are a few centimetres (inches) too high, or the distances as little as 15cm (6in) too short for your horse, you will both end up in a mess. Starting off with small crosses gives you the chance to discover early on if you have measured it badly for your horse, and you can then alter the grid before

any damage has been done. If you have set the jumps so high that you are crashing through the grid, either reduce the height or lengthen the distance. You are trying to tune him up, not wreck him.

This is a very versatile grid, because it can also be used for corrective therapy for careless front legs too. However, if you do use this grid for corrective treatment rather than tuning up, be very careful. Build the grid on a conventional distance of 3.7m (12ft), with small crosses to a true parallel at the end. If your horse has been running a little on

Opposite and above: Millie can sometimes be a little extravagant with her jump and occasionally throws Brenda out of balance. These short, sharp bounces do not give Millie time to exaggerate her jump, making it far more comfortable for both of them.

the forehand and you want to cure him, *gradually* shorten the last distance. (If you want to improve the horse's technique, *always* do it gradually.) If he copes with the shorter distance by snapping up nicely and making an effort to clear the front pole, you have achieved the desired effect for now. You will do even more lasting good if you can shorten the distances all the way back down the line.

If the horse starts to find it too difficult, you must discover why. Is he being lazy or careless, or is he finding himself in an impossible situation? If he is lazy or careless, of course you will persist. But how will you know?

Perhaps it is your own fault for not producing enough impulsion for him to cope with this testing line. Maybe your balance could do with some improvement. Or have you increased the severity of the grid too quickly?

If there is the slightest suspicion that you may be in any way to blame, reduce the grid, and do not build it up again until you have bucked up your riding ability. Why should he try so hard if you are not making the effort?

If the grid is genuinely too difficult because you have been over-ambitious by shortening the distances too quickly, make it easier for yourself by lengthening them again. You should have developed enough affinity with your horse to know if he is distressed or merely idle, so do not force him to struggle. There is no point in putting him off by being much too tough.

This is a grid that needs to be set just so if it is not going to produce an adverse effect by overfacing the horse. This will not be due to the size of the fences – they are not big. It is the distances that will dictate the true severity of the grid by demanding more or less effort according to the length between the jumps. An easier grid will often help restore his confidence, and your enthusiasm to ask for a little more effort can be developed more slowly.

Careful construction of the grid is essential. It is meant to be a tune-up for the genuine horse and a reminder for the schoolmaster to stay well behaved and not become careless, not an impossible task to put them off completely. Do not forget, if you gradually increase the size of the jumps and decrease the distances at the same time, you are doubling the severity of the changes. Change one *or* the other, and only by centimetres (inches). You will recognize if your horse is trying because you will feel more lift. Do not be tempted to ask for too much more, because you will be very close to being unfair and asking the impossible.

An experienced trainer would be a great help in setting up and analyzing the effect and results of using this particular grid. Whether you are using it for tuning up, or as a remedial exercise for you or the horse, a competent observer will be invaluable. He or she will quickly recognize how much to push both of you to get the most benefit from the exercises, and will know when you have done enough. An experienced trainer will also not allow the grid to become so severe that it has the opposite effect to the very one you are hoping to achieve.

The Rushing Horse

Front or back legs, it will not matter which to the horse who is intent on going to his fences too fast. You will hardly have time to decide which of his legs are knocking the poles. He will hit them just as easily with either, and you will have to cure him of rushing before you can then improve his technique. Until he is in a position to listen to your instructions, you will achieve nothing.

Blatant disobedience to your initial suggestions about pace will require a slightly different approach to your gridwork. However subtle and under-standing you may be, however carefully you may prepare a grid to slow him right down, this horse will knock poles down with any leg because he is simply going *too fast*. You can deal with him being a bit keen: high crosses will sort that out.

But being wilful and naughty, carting you into the grid with far too much pace to clear the poles – this is definitely not acceptable!

If the horse is crashing poles, and not seeming to care much either, you must slow him down before you do anything else. Obviously his hind legs are not effective in producing impulsion because he is lugging you along on his forehand. There is no time or room to snap up cleanly, and there is no inclination to co-operate. He is trying to please himself, not to please you.

At this stage, whether the horse is hitting the poles with his front or back legs is immaterial. What is important is that you regain the initiative and have control of the pace. You want him backing off the poles so that you can make him be co-operative from your leg.

Tack Options
You could try using a different bit. Once you increase the severity in his mouth, there is usually no way back, so be resigned: if you are simply out of control, there really is no other option. You must be safe, so be realistic. You are not going to improve the way he jumps at this sort of speed.

If you do need to change to something a little more severe, try a soft mouth three-ring bit for starters. It will give you some adjustment for severity, the mouthpiece will not be harsh, and the slight gag action gives the horse a different feel. He may be less likely to argue. If you try a bit with a curb chain, it could produce a hollowing effect, and your horse might try to fight against it.

If your horse is generally happy in his mouth and only gets into overdrive when jumping, try a Market Harborough martingale. It is a *safe* training aid, and you will not be able to overdo the severity. Side reins or draw reins can be

This page:
Helen's horse is very keen, and she needs some help to steady him to a fence without his fighting her. It is almost impossible for her to use enough leg for impulsion when Zebedee is hollowing so badly against her contact. No Market Harborough equals a high head and dangly legs.

Opposite:
Helen works through the grid using the Market Harborough and discovers that she is in a position to use her legs more effectively, producing impulsion instead of pace. Because the aid works on a leverage principle rather than by introducing a harsher bit, Zebedee is less inclined to try to be evasive. He cannot work out why Helen suddenly has much more control.

positively dangerous when jumping, as they could become entangled with the horse's legs. Do *not* use them!

The design of the Market Harborough will prevent the horse snatching at you and pulling you forward up his neck. It will also give you a different directional pull to stop him hollowing his head and neck in resistance, and you will probably still be able to use the bit that he goes well in the rest of the time. The whole purpose of this aid is to slow him down and allow you to be in the position to get some leg on him and produce more impulsion instead of pace; then you will be able to encourage a much more rounded jump. Do not forget: if you change something to improve the brakes, you require more leg.

There are alternative methods to try to slow down your horse, but they are only mentioned so that you will be able to recognize them and *avoid* using them, as they are mostly unfair to the horse. However frustrating the rushing horse may be, there are no short cuts to curing him, particularly if the methods used carry a higher risk factor than ordinary schooling fences.

Unfair Fences

It is possible to face a rushing horse with jumps that are not entirely fair. The principle is that he will hurt himself by hitting the poles, and back off and try harder to jump them properly next time. Certainly your poles should not be flimsy, as this will only encourage the horse to be causal, but this sort of treatment might have started the trouble in the first place.

If your horse has been frightened by being sent over unfair fences, it could produce two problems: refusals and running away. The horse's natural

A much improved
approach and outline.

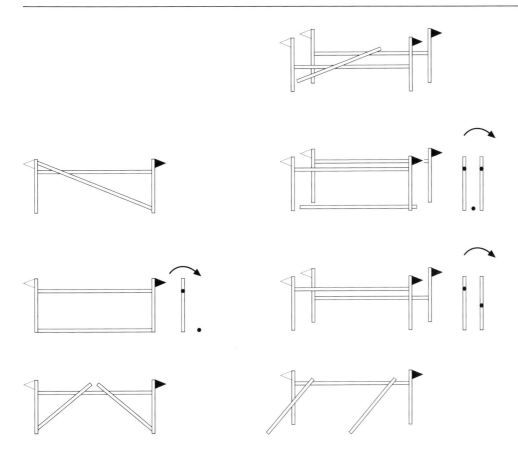

response to fear is to run away. If he is frightened by a jump but bullied quite strongly enough to prevent him stopping, his obvious response will be to hurry, and that could well be the root of your problem. Whatever it is that has caused him to rush in the first place, you will still have to find the remedy, and jumping unfair fences is *not* going to effect a cure.

The British Show Jumping Association (BSJA) rule book illustrates several practise fences that should not be used. One or two examples have become fashionable with some trainers, and of course, they will make some horses back off and jump cleanly, especially if they are incorporated in a grid, but you will not find them in the ring and they are unacceptable as far as safety goes (Fig 14). Some are built with the express

purpose of actively encouraging the horse to hit the pole. False groundlines and wedged poles are easily constructed, and if he hits the jump hard enough, the theory is that he will pick his feet up better next time.

Sometimes it must be tempting to build such jumps, especially if you are getting to the end of your patience with a horse you are sure is being wilfully naughty. Do *not* do it!

The Hit-and-Hurry Cure

Try the 'hit-and-hurry cure' instead (Fig 15).

Hold the horse in trot in the middle of the poles and do not look down at the first double cross. If he still pulls you out of balance, make him walk over the

*Fig 14 Unfair options. These combinations of fences should **not** be used.*

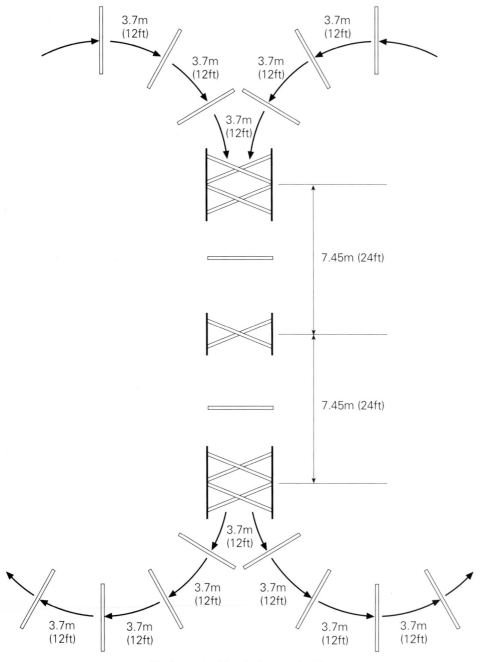

Placing poles identical on each side

Fig 15 The hit-and-hurry cure.

narrower part of the poles, and if he gets over the first jump and picks up too much pace, high cross the placing poles as well. Be ready to scold him if he is careless, and do not let him lug your weight forward. This is when you need a Market Harborough to keep him lighter on the forehand. Do not be dragged to the first fence out of balance, and walk if you have to. Approaching from a short turn will prevent him leaping forward as soon as he sees the grid.

Turn alternate ways when you land, and turn short so that the horse does not get a chance to hook off in gallop. He will settle and be more obedient as he discovers it is easier to jump cleanly from a slower pace, and he should be glad to stop you grumbling each time he hits a pole.

Make the grid look fairly uninviting by keeping the crosses fairly acute, although not too high. Use the placing poles immediately after the grid to help you regain your balance again as quickly as possible to steady way from the jump.

If he is still going too fast to do it properly, do not be disheartened too

The 'hit-and-hurry' grid.

soon. You will need several sessions over this type of grid before you start to get some results. Do not forget: somewhere along the line he has discovered how to go fast, and it will probably be as an evasion from something unpleasant.

Reasons for Rushing

So often young horses showing a lot of talent are rushed along. They are simply not given time to develop a technique, but are just chased to get from one side of the fence to the other. If they are not encouraged to jump by a sympathetic manner, they might refuse, or they might use extra speed to get the jumps over and done with quickly. It is also possible that your horse is being really naughty and choosing to rush as a nap or disobedience.

You must make up your mind what is causing the problem. Whichever it is, you will still need to impose the same sort of quiet discipline to help you get a result. This 'hit-and-hurry' grid will help by changing and steadying the approach, and making it physically easier to clear the poles.

If your horse does become steadier going in but still accelerates on the way through, try adding extra jumps to the line. They need not be higher. Make the distance another 7.45m (24ft) to a single cross, and then to another double cross also on 7.45m (24ft). Put placing poles in the extra distances 3.1–3.35m (10–11ft) from the landing sides, to try to steady him on the way through, and do not forget the placing poles at the end. Add two more on each rein at 3.7m

(12ft) distances in the middle. Then if he is disobedient and turns too wide, he will not make the poles at all and you will recognize that he is still being evasive of your commands.

Perhaps seeing a long grid will steady him a bit more, as it will look like a real jumble of poles to be negotiated. Conversely, if he has really been got at, he might try to rush even more to get it over with. You will know from his response if these extra jumps are going to be helpful or not. Adjust your grid accordingly. If they are making things worse, remove them, but try it four or five times at least before you give up on it.

Be patient. He is already in a hurry, so you certainly do not want to gee him up any more.

Conditions for Improvement

You will not get any improvement until you can produce your horse from your leg. Try any external changes with the bit or gadgets to steady him down; he must accept that your leg is an aid for impulsion, not a 'go fast' signal. Then continue to use this grid until he learns to do exactly what you ask of him.

Hopefully you will find that speed is the entire problem. Once he has slowed down, consistent impulsion into an accepting contact might be all that is necessary to start jumping clear rounds.

Patience and understanding will prevail eventually, but it will take a long time to get his head right. Do not try any short cuts. They may make a temporary improvement, but it will not last!

TEN

Back-leg Bangs

So far we have concentrated on how to improve the four-faultitis in front, but of course, knocking down poles with the back end is just as costly, and maybe not be quite so straightforward to cure.

Hitting poles behind is mainly caused by the rider failing to produce enough impulsion. This leaves the hind leg trailing slightly in the air. Losing your balance in the air does not improve your chances of jumping clear rounds either.

Perhaps you feel your horse is entirely to blame. He might be foolishly bold and misjudging his ability, taking off too far from the fence, or he could be failing to make the spread because he has been too ambitious. This often happens at triple bars. Is it his fault? Probably not! This type of knockdown usually happens because the rider has used a bit too much pace. Pace will not help make up extra width in the air to jump cleanly unless it is backed up by impulsion, and it is easy to misjudge the degree of impulsion you have if you accelerate faster than you are used to going.

Analyzing the Cause
You must build a grid to help overcome the problem. Start off with a small double cross to three small crosses and a double cross to finish, at 3.35–3.7m (11–12ft) distances. Build it so that your

distances are kind and suit your horse's stride. Pop down the grid as it is and take note if there is any hint of carelessness. If he is tapping the small

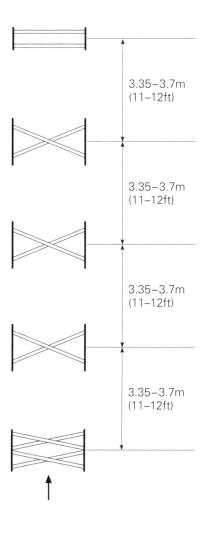

3.35–3.7m
(11–12ft)

3.35–3.7m
(11–12ft)

3.35–3.7m
(11–12ft)

3.35–3.7m
(11–12ft)

Fig 16 Grid for back-leg bangs.

The high cross to placing pole helps Belinda produce enough impulsion to allow Harry to operate well over the parallel, even if he is arguing on the non-jumping stride. Belinda concentrates on holding her position in the air just that split second longer to allow Harry's hind leg time to clear the fence.

crosses, make them high. Leave the end fences small.

Raising the middle crosses will back the horse off and slow him down. By not increasing the distances, he will be rounder and slower in the air, and this will give you a chance to analyze whether it is your balance or a lack of impulsion which is causing the problem. Note if he starts to struggle by the third high cross. If he finds it difficult to keep going and is casual over the last fence, you are lacking impulsion. If he jumps out over the middle crosses with no lack of pace and impulsion, it could be your balance that is causing the lazy back leg.

Your horse might just be careless, and touching poles could be nothing to do with your riding at all, but it *is* your riding that must put it right. Leave the crosses high in the middle and raise the last jump to be a small parallel – not too high, but rather wider than normal (Fig 16). Use plenty of leg but not too much pace as you go through the grid. The small first fence will set you up for the rest of the exercise. Do not worry about your approach to this rather imposing-looking jumble of poles. High crosses always look worse than they are – that is exactly what makes them a very effective exercise for curing carelessness.

Drill yourself to look up through the grid to avoid any tendency to tip. You do not want to develop a front leg problem too. Consciously hang your weight off the stirrup bars and practise and practise letting the knee be soft enough to be an effective shock absorber. Unless you can drop your weight through that knee and let it absorb your motion, your upper body will not be able to stay in the balance necessary to give your horse the freedom to elevate behind. In fact, if you allow your weight to get a bit behind him, you will be actively hindering him to the extent of causing his back leg to drop on the pole.

The high crosses should give you maximum impulsion as the horse's hind leg must be through underneath him, otherwise he will stop. If he does stop, you will know that you have been too far forward with not enough leg, or you have given your contact, or both at the same time! Do it again properly.

When you reach the last jump, it will look comparatively easy both to the horse and to you. If your balance mid-air is wrong, he will hit the jump behind.

Timing

You must be busy with your leg through the grid. You will then *know* that you have plenty of impulsion to tackle the last jump. As the horse jumps it, prepare to hang in the stirrups a bit longer than normal. The jump is wider than you have been practising, therefore he will be in the air that little bit longer, so do not spoil his effort by anticipating the landing and shifting your weight a split second too soon.

Do not change your position in the air one bit; just hold it a little longer to enable your horse's hind leg to be clear

of the poles before you start to come down. This does not require any extra riding ability. After all, it is only a matter of common sense. If your horse's back leg is still over a pole, do not distract him by shifting your weight prematurely. You do not have to ride better to get it right. What you do on the horse isn't different, just better timed.

The 'good boy' syndrome comes into this too. Perhaps you do not like the look of the jump, and fear the horse might not come up. If you collapse with relief because you are actually in the air, he will hit the poles. As you have already discovered, if you collapse immediately your horse takes off, he will hit the fence in front. If you do not feel that surge of relief until you are a bit further through the effort, your collapse will correspond with his hind legs being over the fence.

Whatever causes your shift in weight, whether relief or an error of judgement, you must work very hard to improve this aspect of your jumping.

Increase and Persist

Widen the last parallel even more, although it should still not be too high. You are trying to produce a feeling for the amount of time you are actually suspended over the poles in order to practise waiting in the air for that split second longer. You must allow the horse freedom to be well clear of the spread before you adjust for your descent. Do not let the shift in weight occur too early and distract him.

The effort of waiting in the air must not spoil your contact and impulsion. You must still produce the horse to the fence with no change in effort. All that is required is better timing and balance when you are airborne.

ELEVEN

Too Fast – Four Faults

We have already discussed improving horses who rush their jumps through panic or naughtiness, but what about those horses who are going too fast because they and the rider are just a little too enthusiastic?

Jump-offs

Often a jump-off will bring about a change in style from the rider. It shouldn't, but it does! Horses will hit poles behind and in front because they are asked to go too fast. In a jump-off situation, if your horse is keen and you want to win, it will be very easy to forget your rhythm. If you bustle him along, then try to steady on take-off, your riding will be erratic. He is going too fast to be accurate. If you try to steady, your steadying will be stronger than normal, and it will be very easy to forget to put your leg on when you have a double handful going into the jump. It is most uncomfortable to put your leg on when your horse is already going too fast, but pace is no substitute for impulsion.

Calm your enthusiasm. Unless your horse is in a position to be obedient to your leg, he will tow you into the jump on his forehand. As he takes off he will still be pulling at you. The balance of your leg (non-existent) into your contact (of necessity too strong) will make him

hollow as he takes off. If he does not hit the pole on the way up with his front legs, he will definitely catch it behind. You have no hope of being in balance.

Going faster is not the way to win a class. Rhythm, impulsion and balance are all lost if you try to bustle the horse off his stride. Turning, taking strides out, jumping on the angle – *not* checking – are the skills that will help you win classes with far less chance of hitting the poles, and of course there are variations with the gridwork to enable you to learn how to do it (see Chapter 12).

Very occasionally, you might want to take a chance. If you are in a winning position and left only with a long run to the last fence, go for it! If you get it wrong, you will knock it down, so do *not* get it wrong.

Increasing the Speed

If you really want to go faster, you can use your grid to try to make you more accurate. Use the same structure of grid that improves your horse's hind leg, (see Chapter 10, Fig 16). Build a double high cross going in to make him look and steady, and alter the distances to at least 3.7m (12ft) to give him more room to accommodate the extra speed.

Work him through this grid several times. If you go in at a good pace, do not

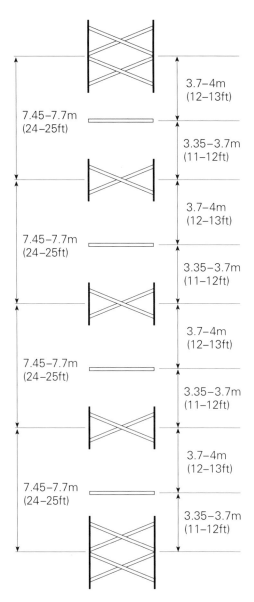

3.7–4m
(12–13ft)

7.45–7.7m
(24–25ft)

3.35–3.7m
(11–12ft)

3.7–4m
(12–13ft)

7.45–7.7m
(24–25ft)

3.35–3.7m
(11–12ft)

3.7–4m
(12–13ft)

7.45–7.7m
(24–25ft)

3.35–3.7m
(11–12ft)

3.7–4m
(12–13ft)

7.45–7.7m
(24–25ft)

3.35–3.7m
(11–12ft)

Placing poles slightly closer to landing side
of each fence

Fig 17 Grid for staying clean at speed.

keep him a little more rounded; you will have that split second longer to stay in balance.

If you are happy with the extra pace, but he is still tanking in on the forehand and tapping the poles, change the grid: double high cross to single to double to single to double on 7.45–7.7m (24–25ft). Put placing poles in between the distances, slightly closer to the landing side of each jump (Fig 17). These will give you more time to balance between the jumps without the horse lugging you forward on the forehand.

This arrangement will steady him slightly, but remember why you have done it – to stop the horse hollowing away from underneath you and to allow you the opportunity to get some leg on. Once you are in that position, you will find he is a bit lighter in the hand. Concentrate on getting your leg on and do this work until he begins to recognize that you are asking for impulsion not pace. The placing poles will prevent him making up too much ground, and the double cross in the middle will certainly make him think.

You must be 'up' on the non-jumping strides. If he does not want to be steadied to back off the jump and stay accurate, he might try to say no. Do not tip forward to give him the choice.

The extra double cross will help you discover just how much time you need to stay in position in the air to give him at least a chance of getting it right. The placing poles will steady him on landing, which will help. Practise hanging in the air for even longer than you think is necessary. However fast your approach, once your horse has learned to back off and jump cleanly, he will be more rounded. Improving his technique will make him that bit slower in the air, and

forget impulsion. You are thinking about holding him off the fence, and if your contact is too strong for the degree of leg, he will hollow and be unable to stay accurate. The high crosses going in should steady him slightly and help you

you will be up there a lot longer than you anticipate. Do not get the timing wrong.

Repeat the grid at a good pace until you feel the improvement, but be very careful about how much you ask. This is an extremely strenuous grid, with five fairly serious jumping efforts, and any progress you make will be lost if you persist in working when either of you are genuinely tired. You want co-operation, not submission.

Do not worry if you feel you have not progressed a lot the first time you try this. It is very difficult for both of you to

Stay clean at speed. Mary and Ryan are well on their way to producing more accurate jumping at speed.

remain accurate with the jumping when you are in a hurry, and requires lots of practice. If you have to stop because your horse has done enough, do not be perturbed because you feel he could have improved more. It will sink in gradually. You can expect the next session to proceed far more smoothly as you get more feel for what you are hoping to produce. After all, you are trying to make it easier for him to do what you want, not more difficult.

Avoiding Confusion

Do not be at cross purposes. Let the poles encourage improvement, rather than you resorting to being too bossy. Only check the horse if he is running on *too* fast. Until he is willing to accept that check without arguing, you will be at odds over your fences. You want to get the jumps right, not start a battle, and you are both keen to get to them. The only possible difference between you is that *you* want to clear them; in the excitement of the extra pace, he might not be too bothered. He will be hollow and careless, particularly with his back end.

You cannot get enough leg on to produce impulsion because the horse wants to interpret your leg as the 'go fast' signal, so he will not have his hind leg in the right place to produce the necessary lift. You will still be trying to steady him and he will be arguing with your contact and hollowing his whole body. Even if he struggles and gets his front end clear, he will make the wrong shape in the air. He will physically be unable to avoid the poles, even if he wants to. Your balance will be wrong

because you will still be trying to steady. Even if you hang well in the stirrups in the air, it will not be effective enough. His hind legs will not be far enough underneath him to get up cleanly.

If your horse enjoys his jumping he will love going faster. So, rather than fighting with his mouth, be a little devious. Let the grid produce the desired effect through its appearance and carefully set distances. Persistence will eventually pay off. You will gradually find yourself being able to go that bit faster while your leg keeps producing impulsion, but the horse has got to remain controllable and careful. Use this grid to feel the correct degree of leg to contact that will keep him accurate.

When you are satisfied, remove the placing poles, one at a time. If you remain fast and accurate, fine. If he starts to flatten again, replace them. Repeat this until you can balance up on the non-jumping stride without their help.

Beginning with the last jump, change the fences one by one to conventional parallels and uprights. If he starts to be careless, change them back to high crosses or use the placing poles again. You may have to do both. Discover what is most effective, and make those poles work *for* you.

If you really want to go faster, it will be very hard work to produce the athleticism and balance essential to avoid hitting poles. Do not expect your horse to stay faultless at speed unless you are prepared to invest time, energy and lots of hard work on the grid.

There are actually better ways of improving your time in a jump-off, without accelerating.

TWELVE

Improving Jump-offs

Gridwork does not always have to be remedial or corrective. Once your horse is jumping clear rounds at shows, your gridwork will give you all the skills necessary to produce quick and accurate jump-offs without going fast and flat and kicking poles out – it is no good having the fastest time if you have galloped round and knocked half the poles down (all pace and no impulsion!). Your jump-offs should be calm and collected and your horse should be the same.

Better times and more accuracy

Your jumping will have progressed to a reasonable standard to enable you to jump the first round clear, and it will not be necessary to lower your standards in an attempt to produce a winning time. Most classes are won by far more subtle methods than just galloping faster.

★ Turning
★ Taking jumps on the angle
★ 'Taking strides out'.

All these will be far more effective than going too fast to remain accurate, and you do not need an extensive range of jumps in order to learn how to produce these skills.

Build a grid of a double cross to three placing poles to another double cross, all on 3.7m (12ft). The poles will help you ride three nice active, rounded strides. Try to position the line against a wall or fence. Work through the grid a few times and gradually build both jumps up to two small *true* parallels. If you are using a mixture of both jumps and make-do supports, the fences *must* be true parallels. Establish a good rhythm in the middle, then remove the placing poles.

Start off with fence A jumped from a diagonal line towards the corner (Fig 18). Do not allow this slightly different approach to put you off. Look for a point approximately 1.85m (6ft) in front of the fence and head for that. The proximity of the wall will square up the horse as you jump and help you take the fence in the middle.

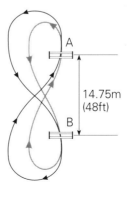

14.75m (48ft)

——— Original route 15 or 16 strides

––––– Short route 10 or 11 strides

Fig 18

If you keep your shoulders level and do not collapse your outside rein, you should land in correct canter. Without 'motorbiking', keep a positive outside contact, turn on a semicircle to prepare to jump fence B. Again, this will be on an angled approach to a point 1.85m (6ft) in front of the jump. How severe that angle will be depends on the size of the semicircle. Try not to drift too far out or the angled approach will be difficult. The wall will help your horse square up to the middle of the jump, but you must not ask the impossible.

Try once more to keep your weight quite level in the air and do not start to anticipate the turn. If you collapse inwards or ease your outside rein too much, you will land disunited. Carry on round and repeat this figure-of-eight exercise. Do not make the loops too tight to start with; you should be riding comfortable semicircles. Try to think about taking 15 or 16 strides around the corner and across to your next jump.

Your horse will soon start to anticipate the turns and think he knows where he is going. As long as you do not let him get too clever and start to motorbike, you will be able to use this attitude to help you reduce the number of strides between the fences. Instead of turning on a semicircle, gradually shorten your effort into a U-turn.

As soon as you have landed, have your eye round the turn and fixed on the next jump, or the point 1.85m (6ft) in front of the jump that you are steering for. If you do not commit your eye to where you want to go, you will be risking a very avoidable glance-off. The wall will guide you on one side, but unless you really concentrate on where you need to steer, the horse will run out, not with any naughty motive but simply because you

have presented him badly to the jump – or in fact to the wing!

It is terribly obvious advice, but let your head swivel to allow your eye to wander well in advance of your actions. So many riders are fixed and rigid in their head and shoulders, and do not quite realize how much advantage can be gained when making up time on a track purely by looking that little bit further ahead. On a turn, be pliable. Do not come away from the jump with your eyes firmly fixed between the horse's ears, as you will not see where you want to go until your turn is complete. You must look much further along your route than that. How can you ride the most beneficial turn and line of approach if you do not look for that line until you are actually round the corner? It will then be too late for any adjustment to your turn. You should have a clear view of where you mean to go: guesswork and an awareness of the position of the next jump will not be nearly good enough. *Look* for it!

Get used to looking further ahead – it is quite useful to see where you are going! You will also have much more warning if any alteration needs to be made to your planned track. Sometimes things go wrong in a jump-off and you may need to deviate from your original plan, and if you are looking well in front you will be able to ride a different route without fussing the horse.

Without going any faster, you should be able to reduce the number of strides between these fences to 10 or 11. As you can see, the saving of time from the original track will be considerable: a saving of at least 10 strides, and several seconds, for the two turns. If you can manage to save this number of strides on each turn in your jump off, you will achieve a very economical time without galloping at all.

Possibilities

Practising this exercise will allow you to discover just how much you can ask from your horse and actually get. It will also reveal any shortcomings in your technique. If you ask for something and do not get it, why?

Analyze why it has not come off. Have you tried to turn so short that you have actually checked to get round? Have you tipped forward and not maintained impulsion from a stay-back position? All your turns *must* be ridden from behind. The second you get in front of the horse on a turn you will lose impulsion. If you tip or lean, the horse's hind leg will not come through far enough underneath him to keep up momentum and any benefit of a tight turn will be lost. Then you will flap and urge him on to the next jump from a forward position. Even if he manages to keep going, he will be unlikely to clear it.

Once you have negotiated the turn, it is very easy to relax and fail to keep up the pressure from your leg. You must keep a good active rhythm all the way through the exercise; practise until you can maintain it all the way round this figure of eight. As soon as you have completed the turn, the line across the next jump should be straight, not wavy. Commit yourself to that point in front of the jump, and ride your horse *straight* to it.

As soon as you have landed, try to concentrate on maintaining the rhythm and impulsion away from the jump. The quicker you can be back in balance, the easier the horse will find it to keep going forward without checking. Do not make him have to check because you have

been too ambitious with your route.

If you do misjudge your inside line, the wall will help you square up to the fence. Even if you jump on a slight angle, it will not matter: it will be extra practise for when you do require an angled approach to get the maximum benefit from a turn.

Of course you will get it wrong to start with. It is only experience and practice that will teach you exactly how much to expect. Just remember why you are practising – to reduce the time taken on a course without going any faster and losing accuracy.

Once you are quite happy with your performance, the exercise can be ridden the opposite way round (Fig 19). This will give slightly different options on the methods used to reduce the time taken.

As you approach the first jump A, you should be trying to get a touch closer to the wall than normal. Look across the point where you want to go on the diagonal. If you are working in a dressage-size arena, look towards the A or C marker. From your approach, encourage the horse to turn very slightly on his take-off stride. Do not confuse

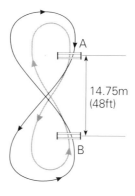

14.75m (48ft)

——— Original route 15 or 16 strides

——— Short route 10 or 11 strides

Fig 19

him by asking for too much angle. As soon as you have landed, on stride one turn a little more, completing the angle necessary for the required line. Ride a straight line across the diagonal, but already be aware of your next turn. Let your eye be drawn to jump B as you go past it, and do not lose sight of it as you turn. Your head can move, so do not let a rigid neck spoil your economy of movement.

As with the original exercise, do not overdo your first few efforts. The turn should start off as a semicircle, and only gradually become more ambitious. It will be a great asset to have the wall helping you into the jump, as it will square you up and stop you exaggerating the angled approach until you are quite ready for it. Practise the slightly angled approach as you carry on through the exercise. Although the wall will help your turn back to the jump, do not ask the impossible. If you try to be too short, it will make your horse put on the brakes and lose rhythm.

It will be trial and error until you feel you have actually produced the best and most economical route. Look for 10 or 11 strides again. If you try to reduce it any further, you will lose impulsion on the turn and not have enough power to clear the jump easily. It is very easy to collapse after the turn and think you have done enough. Do not let the turn or your enthusiasm tip you forward so you lose impulsion.

You have done a good job if your horse accepts all that you ask without suspecting you may be trying to reduce your time. Stay cool and calm. He will only be upset if you bustle him – far better to ensure that he enjoys what you are doing, and finds it easy.

This exercise will help you learn some of the skills involved in riding decent jump-off tracks. It demands turns, angles and reducing the number of strides. Ridden properly, it will give you a good basic understanding of how much you can ask and expect to receive from your horse, and what you receive will be in direct proportion to the consistency of the rhythm and impulsion you maintain throughout the exercise.

Variations

Once you are quite happy and working reliably with these two variations, add two more fences, C and D (Fig 20). Measure the distance from the middle of A to the middle of D and from the middle of B to the middle of C to be 18.45m (60ft), or four non-jumping strides. Make the extra jumps uprights. It is the route you are concentrating on at the moment, not the severity of the fences.

Start off as you did with the two fences, by jumping A from the diagonal into the corner. Do not turn too tightly to begin with and be very aware of looking far enough ahead for your route. Make your turn a semicircle that is deep enough for your eye to line up the middle of the upright C to the left of the middle of the parallel B. Do not cut the corner to the upright or you will not be in line for B, and will be very likely to glance off the parallel.

Try to ride a straight line across the diagonal to the left-hand side of the parallel. Looking for the point about 1.85m (6ft) in front of the jump will help you with the steering and make you keep a consistent feel with the left rein. However much you try to keep the horse straight, if you look to the middle he will try to hang in a little. If you are not aware of the tendency to hang inwards to the right, you will soon learn the hard way. Slightly exaggerate your steering to the outside to compensate for this tendency. Obviously your horse will not jump into the wall, so it will not hurt to keep him over a bit to ensure that he is not in a position to run out the other way. If you do head straight to the middle of the parallel, you will find your leg alarmingly close to the wing as he takes off – unless he runs out first.

As soon as you are airborne your eye should already be assessing the route round your next turn. Again, do not cut the corner too sharply. You might succeed in jumping the upright D well, but you will be on the wrong line to the next parallel A and a glance-off will be almost inevitable. If you get it wrong, four strides is hardly time or room for an adequate correction. Exaggerate the steering to the outside again. Jump the parallel A to the right of middle, and remember this when you repeat the exercise.

As you start to flow on and get the idea of the turns, it will be all too easy to collapse the new outside hand across the diagonal if you anticipate the turning after the jump. Keep your shoulders level as you jump the parallels or you will land disunited or on the wrong leg. Be very positive and supportive with the outside rein or the horse will motorbike, leaving you with no impulsion when you square up to the next jump.

You should be trying to maintain the same rhythm all the way round the figure of eight, gradually reducing the number of strides taken by turning a little shorter. Ride consistently into the jumps – it is very easy to get a nice short turn and then relax and stop riding with your leg. You will end up putting in a short stride, losing momentum, impulsion and

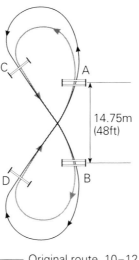

—— Original route, 10–12
   strides round loop
Distance D to A 18.45m (60ft)
Distance C to B 18.45m (60ft)

—— Short route, 7–9
   strides round loop
Distance D to A 17m (55ft)
Distance C to B 17m (55ft)

Fig 20

the rhythm away from the jump.

While you are doing this particular exercise, occasionally go in a straight line from parallel A to parallel B just to make sure the horse is listening to you and not automatically twisting and turning out of habit.

Use your head. You can see from the diagram that there is no point at all in cutting the corner too sharply and taking the uprights on the angle, as this will simply give you a crooked route across to the parallels. You might save a stride on the take-off side of the upright, but you will then need extra strides after landing to retake the track across to the parallel – a complete waste of time! You also run the real risk of a runout at the parallels. Do not take a jump on the

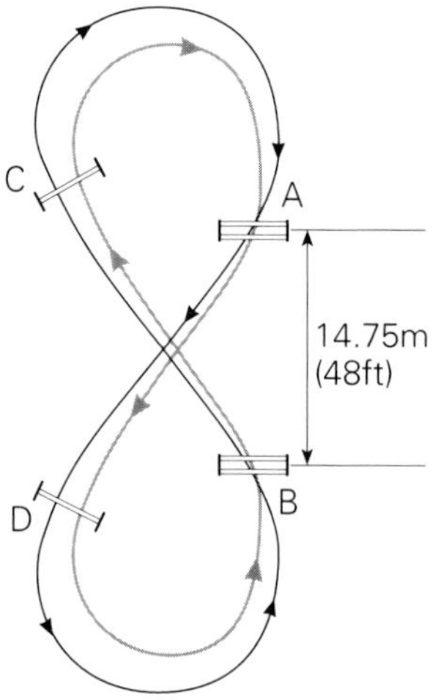

——— Original route, 10–12
strides round loop
Distance A to D 18.45m (60ft)
Distance B to C 18.45m (60ft)

——— Short route, 7–9
strides round loop
Distance A to D 17m (55ft)
Distance B to C 17m (55ft)

Fig 21

angle if there is no advantage to be gained. In this particular case it would be a positive hindrance.

You must learn when to be clever and when to be conservative. This exercise will help you learn exactly how much you must ask to direct your horse round the shortest route taking the least number of strides. The opposite exercise will help you develop slightly different skills (Fig 21).

Start at A and ride the route a few times with fairly wide turns to get your eye in. Jumping from the parallel A across to the upright D needs a very different preparation to do the shortest route. You have already practised a slightly angled approach to the parallel, so take the same approach but be looking across to the upright D. Land,

and on stride one complete the angle necessary to ride the straight line across to the middle of the upright. Do not ride a wavy line. Commit your eye to the correct route and stay on it. You should already be sighting on to and round the turn to the parallel B.

Your rhythm now is of the utmost importance. As soon as you have landed, re-establish that rhythm so that your turn has power and impulsion and you can turn as short as you like. The wall will guide you round to the jump, so make use of it to keep the pressure on. Just keep the horse coming through underneath you and your turn can be as ambitious as the impulsion produced. If you lose impulsion you will literally run out of steam, he will drop back from underneath you and you will be very lucky to gather him up again to get over the jump, so do not ask for more turn if *you* cannot produce the power.

As you approach parallel B, you should again be producing the slight angle which will give the best line across the diagonal to C. Now you can start to angle the upright. Instead of taking the jump squarely, be very conscious of the right turn you will have afterwards. You can turn as sharp as your impulsion allows after C, because the wall will help guide you round the corner. Head for the right-hand side of the jump. Be prepared to use a little more outside leg to stop your horse drifting to the left, and be ready to have that outside leg firmly pushing you round as soon as you have landed.

There is another element to consider if you choose this route. Because you are jumping C to the right, the distance between B and C will be slightly shorter than 18.45m (60ft). If you have been popping the jump in the middle from a

perfect take-off point, then you must take a little more hold when you move across to the right-hand side. Steady slightly to allow for the shorter distance, and the sooner the better: it is far better for stride two or stride three to be held up a touch than stride four, immediately before take-off. This will mean the difference between jumping cleanly or tapping a pole, so do not forget to do it.

Using your Head

It is not all physical exertion. Sometimes you have to get your brain in gear as well, and it will need to operate quickly if your jump-off does not go as smoothly as planned. If things go wrong and a turn does not come off, there is no need to go to pieces. You should be sharp enough to have an alternative mind, and use it!

If you choose to jump C on the angle, there will be fewer strides and less time round to parallel A. If your eye is not looking far enough ahead, you will be caught out by arriving at parallel A a little sooner than expected. Do not jump the parallel angling the wrong way, towards the wall rather than away from it.

As soon as you land from C, your eye should be preparing you to ride the

Lesley is producing Candy on a perfectly angled jump to ride the best possible line across to the next fence.

correct line from A to D. However quickly you come to the parallel, you should still be looking far enough ahead to where you are meant to be going, particularly if you want to jump upright D on the angle too. If you do not look, you will not make it!

Do not check to give yourself more time to look where you are going. You know you can ride at the same time as looking for your route, so do not waste time unnecessarily.

This is just the sort of exercise to practise to help you acquire jump-off skills. Vary the track so that occasionally you go in a straight line to both parallels. In fact, you can make up quite a long course using only the four jumps.

Four-fence Track
The twists and turns on this track (Fig

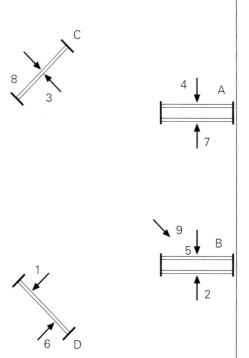

Fig 22 Four-fence track.

22) give you every opportunity to practise staying balanced and maintaining a rhythm. Do not get dizzy! It is very hard work for both of you to do it properly and involves mental concentration as well as physical exertion.

When you are quite confident of producing some decent work, move the whole grid over away from the wall. Still have everything set at exactly the same distances, but without the wall to help guide your chosen track. Now you will need to be a little more accurate with your line over the parallels.

On the first exercise (Fig 20), your line from the upright must be perfect. If you cut the corner to the upright at C, you will runout at the parallel B to the inside. If you take the upright C square on but fail to produce a line right to the middle of the parallel B, you will glance off to the outside. You cannot use the point in front of the parallel to guide you, because there is no wall to square you up to the jump. You must head straight for the middle and take the parallel on the angle, pointing slightly across to the left. With no wall to square you up, you must rely on a little more outside leg, and be very careful to keep a consistent contact to the fence. Any hint of fiddling with your hands will spoil your approach.

Have the confidence to ride the line without changing your mind and trying to adjust the steering when you should already be committed: it will be too late to change the route without messing up your balance and rhythm. If you tip even the slightest bit too far forward, your horse will be distracted at this angle and be actively encouraged to run out. If you get it right, you will land angled slightly away from the turn. Be extra sharp in balancing up and use a slightly stronger outside leg to stop him drifting too far over out of the turn. If you try to steer him without using your legs to help, he will motorbike and lose impulsion round the turn to D. Be level as you land so that you can assume the 'up' position with your body as quickly as possible – that is, immediately! Do not allow him to run too wide just because there is no wall to help you turn, and do not let him lean in underneath you.

Complete the figure-of-eight exercise, trying to take the same number of strides round the turns at each end. Do not be surprised if your horse finds one rein easier than the other. Try to bring the poorer side up to scratch, but remember his natural inclinations. In the ring it is possible to make use of this knowledge; be a little more ambitious if you know it is a turn that will suit him, and perhaps a little more cautious if you know it is not the favoured side. Again, use your head.

The second exercise (Fig 21) presents you with other options. Steering a touch wider on the approach to A and angling a little more into the parallel will give you a better line into the upright D. If you jump D on the left, remember the distance will be slightly short and allow for balancing and steadying slightly on stride two or three across the diagonal. A better angle there will shorten the distance to get round the turn again for the next jump, the parallel at B.

Try to take as few strides as possible without losing rhythm and impulsion. If you find your horse checking and losing momentum, you are turning too short and losing impulsion. If you kick him on too fast, he will be going too wide on the turns and losing whatever advantage the angled jump has given you. Look for power not pace, and however short you want to turn, do not be too ambitious with the route and let it spoil his particular rhythm.

This particular set-up of your grid fences will give you all the skills necessary to do fast times in jump-offs without using so much pace that the horse becomes careless. If you are popping the jumps very neatly and economically from a powerful stride, you will be less likely to have knockdowns. Too fast, and your turns will deteriorate. Instead of a balanced, active canter with plenty of impulsion for nice short turns, you will make long, swooping loops which waste far more time than the extra pace will ever make up.

Practise this set of exercises to make you proficient. Learn how much pace to ask for; discover what sort of angles you can actually manage without running out, and how much impulsion is essential to keep the rhythm going round a tighter route. You will not always win competitions, but at least it will look as if you know how to!

THIRTEEN

Obedience in a Jump-off

You are not going to do well in a jump-off if your horse is argumentative. A clever horse will try to decide for himself where he should be going, and he will not always get it right.

Often you see a horse in a jump-off trying to take the original track. Instead of landing and listening to the rider, he refuses to turn. He wants to go straight on and jump the fences in the same order as the previous round. Once the rider manages to persuade him round the turn and he is presented with a new jump, he is fine. As soon as he is sighted on a fresh fence, he is more than willing to do it.

Sometimes on the way round, the clever horse will mistake the instructions and fix on a jump himself – *any* jump will do for this horse! He will not mind if it is not in the right order: take-your-own-line classes will suit him just fine.

Whatever is causing this complete lack of attention to the rider, it must be put right. The horse must learn to listen and co-operate instead of thinking he knows best.

Often the horse is just keen. Maybe the rider's attitude has hotted him up a little too much to be co-operative. He is quite obviously not reluctant or nappy because he is trying to get to a jump. He just does not comprehend that not any jump will do. Taking his own line is not

acceptable, and he must be encouraged to listen and be more amenable to the steering. He may well want to jump fences, and probably does it very well, but your jump-offs may then become spectacularly unsuccessful as so much time and effort will be wasted in the arguments. You are hardly going to clock a reasonable time if he swoops cheerfully from one end of the ring to the other, oblivious to your efforts to turn him.

The 'Every Which Way' Grid

There is a grid which will help *him* to be more co-operative and *you* to be better and sharper with the steering. Set up a grid of three bounce fences on 3.35m (11ft) – single cross to single cross to double cross – and then three strides to a single cross A on 13.5–14.75m (44 48ft). Build two more single crosses, B and C, on the angle to A, and still on 13.5–14.75m (44–48ft) (Fig 23).

Do not make the angles too acute to start with. Work up the grid in a straight line over A from either rein, and then concentrate on looking exactly where you mean to go. When your horse is warmed up, work over the three bounce jumps and turn left to B. Because he is used to going straight on, he will probably argue, so be prepared.

As you are going over the bounces,

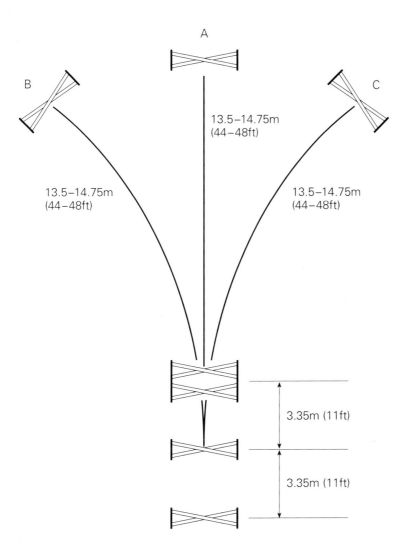

A

B

C

13.5–14.75m
(44–48ft)

13.5–14.75m
(44–48ft)

13.5–14.75m
(44–48ft)

3.35m (11ft)

3.35m (11ft)

look ahead to the new direction. You will want to be turning left after B to come round to the grid again, so a square approach is best. As you take the last bounce jump, land and take a positive feel with your steering. Do not let the horse tip you forward as he tries to ignore your instructions. Do not drop your left shoulder as you land after the parallel, keep your weight well down into stirrup and use a strong right leg to kick him over. You will not get him round with just your reins – your leg must

reinforce the steering too. He is not really being that naughty, just a little arrogant in thinking he knows best.

If you have a problem getting the horse on to the diagonal approach, slow down if possible to give yourself a bit more time to be better organized. He has probably jumped the double cross big in his know-it-all style and you are not sufficiently recovered to take charge of the pace, so drop the bounce fences to the ground if you have to and just trot over them – anything to give you room

Fig 23 The 'every which way' grid.

and time to insist on his making the diagonal approach to B. You are trying to make him co-operate with the steering, not improve his jumping, so do not make the jumps too big.

Even if you have to pull him up to turn across, do so. If you mean to jump the left-hand fence, he *must* do it. Just make sure that there is no misunderstanding. The angle is not deviating that much from the straight line, so it should not be too difficult to make him co-operate.

If he does keep on insisting on towing you in a straight line to A, make A unjumpable, by putting a pole on the top of the wings to act as a barrier. Try anything to make him concentrate and be more willing to listen to you.

Once you have managed to steer him over B, turn away to the left, and come round to the three bounces again. This time turn right to C. Use the same methods to ride your line. If he is still getting away from you with a huge jump over the double cross, make it a single and even smaller. You will be able to build it up again when he is listening.

Whatever sort of jump you get out of the bounces, it is imperative to be in balance immediately again on stride one after landing. Stride two will be too late: he will already have decided which jump he wants to tackle. Your instructions have got to be clear and quick. Do not collapse on landing and allow him the time to choose for himself. Turn right after C and come round to the grid again.

He will soon get the hang of it. Change rein alternately at first. As he gets a little smoother and more co-operative, make the first cross into a small upright. Leave the middle cross alone and make the double cross into a small *true* parallel. The angled jumps B and C can be made into uprights, too.

When you have successfully repeated the exercises enough times to convince you that he is listening, change them. Do not change the rein alternately, but vary it. It is possible that he has automatically anticipated the way you want to go; he might feel relaxed and rather cosy with the alternate rein changes and lose concentration, so keep both of you on your toes. Come the same way two or three times before altering the direction, then next time maybe just once before changing again. It is your signals he must obey, not a preconceived pattern of work.

When you think you have done enough to make sure he is listening, make the angles of B and C slightly more acute so that the turn will be sharper. Incorporate jump A again and switch your exercises to include the straight approach to A as well. If he prefers to carry straight on over A and loses a bit of concentration with your signal to the angled jumps, blank it off again. He must listen and behave.

Just make sure you have not caused him to revert by not making your signals crystal clear. The horse is not really being naughty, just a bit of a know-all. It would be a very different matter if he were evading the jumps or trying to run out. He simply thinks he knows best. It would therefore be unproductive to bully him, and might make him start refusing to go at all. Persist with this twisting and turning from alternate reins until you are sure he is genuinely co-operating.

Different routes
When you reach this stage, there are other route options. All the routes need to be ridden with the specific purpose of ensuring that he listens to and obeys your directional instructions, so of course, your signals must be clear.

Jump up the grid, turn left across to B, then turn right-handed down over C and back through the bounces. The parallel in the bounces must be a *true* parallel, as you will be jumping it from both directions in the same exercise.

The horse will be bound to be surprised at turning the opposite way after B. If you have done enough of the previous work to make him obedient, he should co-operate. He will be even more surprised to jump C backwards and tackle the bounces from the opposite direction. Look exactly where you mean to go and have enough right leg on to help prevent him glancing off the parallel to the right. It is a very real possibility, so be alive to the potential problem.

Do this exercise again from the other way, turning right to C and then left-handed over B and back through the bounce section again.

From the diagram, you can see that taking the return upright on a slight angle will set you up better for the line down to the bounces. Let your eye travel far enough ahead of you to prevent a runout. If you are looping at the top of the grid to turn back down it, it will help to jump the upright away from the bounces on the angle too. Produce a U-turn rather than a semicircle between B and C.

Once you feel you have got it right, alternate this exercise with the original ones. Change the route away from both B and C, randomly alternating either left or right. Then either loop at the top of the grid and return back down it, or go straight back to the beginning directly after jumping just one angled fence.

Variety is essential. Vary your exercises to keep the horse concentrating. Do not make a pattern of turning in the same order, or he will be bright enough

to pick it up. He has got to learn to obey your instructions, so make a random choice of routes. You are trying to cure him of being too clever, so do not give him the chance of slipping into a cosy routine. Just be sure in your own mind that you have a plan, and know which way you mean to go.

Once you are sure you are in control of the steering, bring jump A into the picture again. Ride up the bounces and keep a straight line on over A. As long as you land in balance and give clear directional signals from a stay-back position, you will be able to turn to either B or C and back down the grid. You will also be able to do this in reverse. The loop at the top will obviously need to be tighter if you want to get the best line back down to the parallel, but he will be ready for something a little more testing. It will do you both good!

Play with this grid, choosing the routes at random, and always trying to keep him alert and willing to co-operate. Have the route you want clearly in your head: a moment of indecision, and you will find he will be delighted to take control again.

Do not allow yourself to get slovenly. Ride the horse consistently into your contact, with no tipping or collapsing on the non-jumping strides. Keep him balanced and active, riding all your turns with the weight deep into the stirrups, not over his shoulder. If you exaggerate the signalling with your bodyweight, you will lose impulsion.

Subtle body language
Gradually you will find your horse picking up on your body signals without their being emphasized. If your eye is firmly fixed on the direction you mean to

Sarah chooses a route back down the 'every which way' grid.

take, however hard you try to keep your balance neutral there will be a very slight inclination to the way you want to go. It *must* stay very slight; do not try to develop it. Your horse will sense what it means, but it will be so slight that you will still be balanced enough to ride him properly. Do not fling your weight too far forward over his shoulder as he jumps in an effort to signal the way you want to go.

Of course you must look where you intend to go in the air and allow yourself to give a slight extra feel in the contact for the direction required, but make it subtle. The second you try to wriggle in the direction you mean to take, you will drop your weight one-sided and too far up his neck, and land unbalanced. Then it will be all hand and not enough leg to produce the turn.

You must ride your horse underneath you, and produce your steering from a stay-back position. Let your legs help

you steer; a strong outside leg nudging well behind the girth will be very effective in helping you round the corner, but you simply will not be able to do that if you are forward.

Making progress

As in all gridwork, look for a gradual improvement. Do not increase the severity of the exercise until the horse is totally happy and co-operative with what you are asking. Do not make the jumps too big when it is the steering that needs most attention. Baffle him into co-operating by constantly changing your route and always give clear signals in plenty of time for where you want to go.

There are at least eight variations to this track, so you will be able to keep going for quite a long time without repeating yourself. If you or the horse start to get physically tired, have a breather, finish on a good note, and leave progress to another session.

FOURTEEN

The Square Grid

We have already built a grid to help the argumentative horse learn to be more compliant with the steering, but failing to negotiate the correct track in an economical manner is not always the horse's fault, particularly in a jump-off. Sometimes it is the rider's reactions that are far too slow. The horse may be more than willing to co-operate, but is left directionless because of the rider's lack of co-ordination.

Signals too Slow

A confused horse will rapidly learn to give up. Why shouldn't he? If the rider is too slow to give the signals, whatever is the horse to do?

If you find that you are trailing far behind everyone else in a jump-off, although your horse is more than willing, you must try to do something constructive about it. Be very positive, and learn to transfer your wishes into instructions he can understand more quickly. Of course he will be able to sense some of the time what you want, but he cannot be expected to read your mind successfully enough to do it all for you, especially if you are not quite in tune with the situation yourself.

Jump-offs can and do bring out the very worst in some riders. The word itself is enough to send them into a

panic, and their common sense just disappears. As soon as they get in the ring they go to pieces. The legs freeze, the hands flap, and the track is forgotten. If this happens to you, you must learn to trust yourself a little more. Do not panic – do something about it.

Plan what you mean to do and have a very clear vision in your head of the route you want to take. Develop a more consistent physical co-ordination with your brain. Quite obviously you are reasonably competent, or you would not be jumping clear rounds. Brainwash yourself to ride jump-offs in *the same way* and do not allow yourself to be at all distracted and waffle round the ring. The horse does not want to think you are a different rider because you have changed your style. He will be confused, and unless your instructions are given quickly and clearly, be unable to perform to the best of his ability.

The Square Grid

This grid (Fig 24) will help you sharpen up your reactions and ride a planned route to order. Set on a square, there will be no danger of your horse becoming muddled. If you fail to give him his instructions quickly enough after jumping through one double, all that will happen is he will go straight on. You

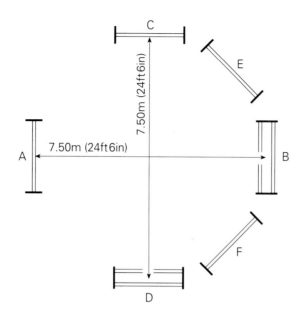

Fig 24 The square grid – sharpen up the rider as well as the horse.

each direction. The extra two fences, E and F, will be used later after you have established that you can cope with the square.

It must be stressed that this is not a grid built as remedial treatment for a naughty horse. Rather, it is a grid to wake up the panic-stricken, lazy or badly co-ordinated rider. Knowing in which direction you mean to go has to be physically indicated by your aids as instructions your horse will understand.

Start on the right rein from A to B (Fig 25). Make an unhurried and square approach, looking across the grid in a straight line. You will find that your horse will then anticipate the direction required afterwards and probably land in left canter. This will suit you perfectly. Turn left, and from a wide three-quarter circle jump across from C to D.

There is something about this grid which encourages the horse to anticipate a change of rein. He will not expect to land and keep coming round in the same direction. That would not be the normal way of schooling, so he will automatically think 'change' and you will probably land in right canter again, ready for the next turn.

If you land on the wrong leg, before continuing the exercise go back to trot and then re-establish correct canter again. Repeat the exercise two or three times, gradually reducing the size of the three-quarter circles. Think far enough ahead on this figure of eight, still being very careful to present your horse squarely to each double. Do not be in a hurry yet.

Now change the route (Fig 26). Start on the right rein and jump B to A, then go left-handed on the three-quarter circle to jump D to C. Take just as much care in thinking ahead and presenting

will not be putting him in an intolerable position because of a lack of steering.

The grid needs to be set up in a fairly wide area to allow you as much scope as possible to get your loops right. As you can see, the jumps are set out in a square, with two additional fences across the corners. Start with crosses and make them the same height all round, as you will want to jump both doubles from

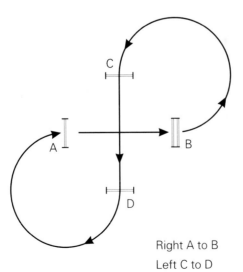

Right A to B
Left C to D

Fig 25

the horse with clear instructions as you gradually shorten the route. Once your horse is warmed up, make the jumps into small uprights and true parallels.

Start the next exercise (Fig 27) on the left rein from B to A, then go right-handed round to C to D. Repeat the same exercise three or four times, really concentrating on your steering, and not allowing the horse to swing out too wide. Then go left rein A to B and right-handed D to C (Fig 28).

These exercises will give you all the variations available for changing rein each time, so practise them until your turns are well organized and assured.

So far the grid has appeared to be uncomplicated and your horse has not needed too much from you in the way of directional skill. He is at least halfway to realizing which way to go. You should be landing mostly in correct canter as he works it out for himself. Do not throw him on to the wrong leg by leaning in on the doubles. If you collapse or tip and drop your new outside hand, he will lean too and be unable to bring the correct hind leg into action properly. Try to be straight as you land, while still indicating with a slight feel to the contact while airborne which way you intend to go – not easy! Only practice will improve your ability.

So far, the exercise work has been fairly straightforward. Practice and repetition of the exercises has allowed you to develop a reasonably short line from double to double. However many strides you originally used on the three-quarter circles, starting off perhaps with as many as 20, you should have reduced that to around 11 or 12 without losing rhythm. All you have had to do is remember where you are meant to be going, and tell your horse. You will know

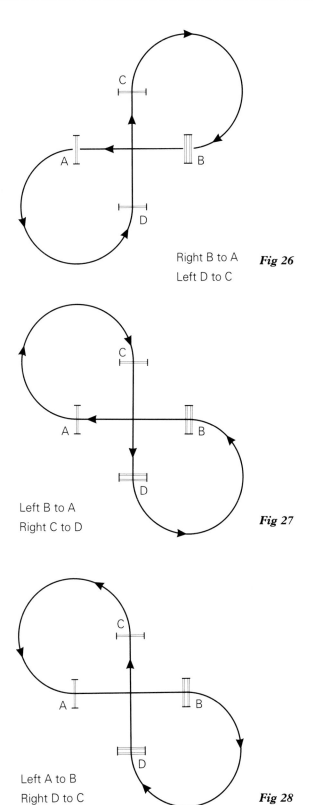

Right B to A
Left D to C   *Fig 26*

Left B to A
Right C to D   *Fig 27*

Left A to B
Right D to C   *Fig 28*

if you are improving when you start the next set of exercises. If your horse has been doing all the thinking for himself, you will be caught out!

More Advanced Exercises

Prepare to tackle the square going over all four doubles from the same rein, using a three-quarter circle to each fresh approach. So far your horse will have anticipated more or less correctly in which direction you want him to go. He will almost be on automatic pilot, so he is certainly not going to expect to be asked to turn on the same rein every time.

Concentrate on the route. Start off on the right rein, and sit up very squarely across the one-stride double. Because of your previous exercises, as well as a natural inclination to do so, your horse is going to expect to turn left. If you have a very clear picture in your mind, if you are thinking ahead and if you are physically able to reproduce what you are planning, you will be able to signal your intentions loud and clear. Ask for another right turn.

Do not collapse your left rein. Make sure that you are looking to the right and ride at least one straight, level stride away from the jump. If you land in left canter, trot and balance up into right canter again. Steer your horse very positively to the right and keep coming round to the next double across the square.

Again, as you jump out, give clear steering signals to the right without unbalancing the horse. Do not give too much with the left rein and over-compensate with the steering. If you try to signal the turn by leaning too far in the air, your horse will only land unbalanced. Have more of a subtle right feel in the contact while you are both airborne, not a wrench! Be kind – remember, this is a nice co-operative horse who is only waiting to be told where to go. He is not trying to argue or dictate the direction. As long as he is told where to go in time, he will be very amenable to your instructions. Get this right, reproduce the same skills in the ring, and your next jump-off will provide much stiffer opposition for your fellow competitors.

As you keep coming round on the same rein, your signals will improve with practice. Do not be in a hurry. A steady improvement will last longer.

If you land on the wrong leg, go back to trot to re-establish the correct leg and rhythm. You are trying to produce clear steering signals with the right hand and remain supportive with the left rein. If you give the outside rein too much, your horse will be unbalanced and lean in on the turn. If the strength of either contact is wrong your horse will be confused.

Clear thoughts and signals

You are hoping that the horse will pick up all the slight body signs that he will be feeling. Your head will be turning to look to the right. He will sense that. You will be a little quicker to feel the contact and steer him, again while still in the air, and your weight might just start to shift very slightly to the right.

Be exceptionally careful not to exaggerate any little hints that involve a shift of weight. If you wriggle, he will be distracted and land unbalanced. Just *thinking* right or left will eventually be enough to alert him as to which way to go. The very tiny, almost unconscious signals that go with your thoughts will warn him, but you have got to think these thoughts in time.

If you waffle about, concentrating only on the jumps, you will land with no clear plan of where you are meant to go next. Your earlier gridwork exercises should have made you reasonably competent by now in producing balance, rhythm and impulsion – almost good enough to feel automatically how your horse is going underneath you without thinking too much about it, leaving you free to concentrate on where you are meant to be going, not on what you are actually doing.

Think ahead! In a jump-off, you are not going to clock up a good time if your horse has run on two or three strides after a jump before you actually tell him which way to go. As you think a bit quicker and plan your track to be tighter, you and your horse will become more in tune. Your signals will be clear but subtle, and he will be well prepared on landing for any particular direction you ask for.

Use this grid to ask for turns the horse is definitely not expecting. If you do not tell him in time he will go the wrong way, so at least you will know who is to blame and how to cure it. Think far enough ahead, look far enough ahead: just doing one good turn will not be sufficient if you go to pieces at the next one.

This is an ideal grid for practising jump-off turning skills as each turn will be round three-quarters of a circle. Not only will the speed and consistency of your steering signals improve, but you will also be practising the sheer economy of movement by taking strides out.

Do the same exercises on the left rein, working your way round the square. Concentrate on riding your horse into the outside hand for balance and impulsion, while giving clear steering signals for your turns. As in the previous exercise, if your signals are subtle and unexaggerated, then your horse will eventually tune in to sense what you want. Just make sure you keep asking.

If you think and look far enough ahead, the signals will become almost automatic. It will not happen immediately, but given time and practice your partnership will become much closer. Your horse will be pleased to receive direction, and your jump-off times will improve.

Varying the route

When you are landing in correct canter most of the time on both reins, start to vary the route. Incorporate figure-of-eight changes, as well as two or three turns all on the same rein. Make sure you plan the route through three or four doubles, and try to remember where you mean to go, otherwise you will not know if you have got it right or not!

If you start to get casual, so will your horse. Whether you change rein or keep turning in along the same direction, the number of strides on your three-quarter circles can be reduced from a fairly comfortable 15- or 16-plus to around 10 or 11, as long as your reactions and signals improve.

You will be able to keep reaffirming your improvement. If your signals are immediate and clear on landing, your horse will go the right way economically with the very minimum of fuss. If your reactions are too slow, your horse will have to decide for himself and will either turn the wrong way completely or go much wider on the turn than necessary.

You will then need to practise these exercises several times to feel a marked improvement, but you *will* gradually become more proficient. Only when you are sure that the horse is listening to you,

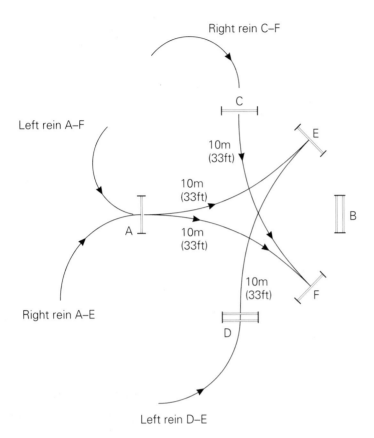

Straightforward approaches

Right rein C–F

Left rein A–F

10m
(33ft)

10m
(33ft)

10m
(33ft)

10m
(33ft)

C

E

B

A

F

D

Right rein A–E

Left rein D–E

Fig 29 Square grid variations. The addition of fences E and F provides a far wider range of options, emphasizing particularly the need to land and steer very accurately on stride one.

*Opposite:
Teresa and Cyril angling through the square grid A to E.*

and that you are giving him the right instructions, should you progress to using the two extra jumps, E and F.

As you can see from the diagram (Fig 29), the fences are set to allow 10.15m (33ft) distances, from A to E, A to F, D to E and C to F, all on two short strides. They can all be ridden from either direction, but great care needs to be taken in the middle of the square. Unless you are very clear in your mind about the route, and very much in physical command of the direction, your horse will just carry on across the square and do the jumps he has become used to.

Plan to start with A to E, then a left-hand turn right round to A again and

across to F. Coming in on the right rein to A will give you the easiest line across the middle; you will be able to take A on the slight angle. Your turn after landing need not be too sharp to get the right direction across to E. Look exactly where you want to go and ride where you are looking.

As you jump A, you must already be pointing across the grid to E. Your horse will be looking for B unless you signal the change of route plainly. You have only two strides in which to get it right, so make sure stride one counts. Be immediately into the 'up' position and riding positively into your contact. You should already be thinking and looking beyond E and planning your left-hand landing.

Do not exaggerate your aids as you tell your horse which way to go. Wrenching him over because you have left the signal too late is not an option. If you are running out of space, it is *your* fault, not his. Have a clear mental vision of your own route and develop the knack of transferring it into fairly quick, concise instructions. Do not be slow to react. Your horse is waiting to find out which way to jump out and exactly where he is expected to go afterwards. If you waffle, so will he. He has no alternative.

Ride a fairly economical line round to A. Keep your inside shoulder up to stop the horse motorbiking and keep pushing him into the outside contact for rhythm and impulsion. As you steer with the inside rein, it is imperative to keep his hind leg coming through for a short and slightly angled approach back to A.

Jumping from A to F will be quite straightforward, as you are approaching from the left rein and already looking through the grid for the most beneficial line. Jump A on the angle so that you

Brenda and Millie going the opposite way, E to A.

1

2

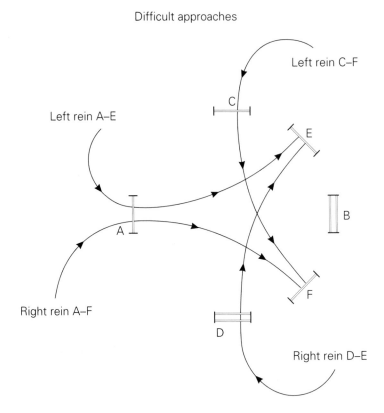

Difficult approaches

Left rein C–F

C

E

Left rein A–E

A

B

Right rein A–F

F

D

Right rein D–E

Fig 30 More difficult tracks through the square grid.

are already almost pointing to the middle of F as you land. Consciously look where you mean to go, and ride the two strides with assurance. Your horse will appreciate it.

You can see from the diagram that the extra two fences give several new route options. Plan a sequence of seven or eight jumps and do them from a good rhythm. Include the one-stride doubles from the first original square. If your instructions are clear and quickly given, you will go where you mean to. It will be most unfair on a very willing and co-operative horse to be indecisive and get him in a muddle. You will always know when your instructions have been late or unclear – your horse will give you away!

More advanced tracks
This is an exceptionally beneficial grid

for a more advanced horse. Do the same exercises, possibly over bigger jumps. Practise control, balance, angles, and reducing the number of strides round the corners.

There are also one or two other routes to be ridden which will need greater control. Do not attempt these if you have only recently started to improve. They are very difficult to do properly, and unless you are confident you can manage easily, do not try them yet. You will only succeed in confusing your poor horse.

Approach the double A to F on the more difficult line from the right rein (Fig 30). Instead of easily producing the correct angle going into and away from A to set you up for F, the difficult approach will positively put you off. Unless you ride it exceptionally well, you will be thrown wide in the wrong direction and probably on to the wrong leg as well. Your horse will have to be very obedient and co-operative to be able to balance and turn so extensively on just two strides, and you will have to be 100 per cent sharp and clear with your directions.

To produce an easier line from a right-hand approach, take an extra stride or two further round before turning into A, so that you are at least square to the fence. This will leave you with not quite as much adjustment to make as if you had cut the corner to A. Try the same exercise going left-handed C to F, left-handed A to E and right-handed D to E. If you turn in short to any of these, the lines across the middle will be very difficult.

Learn how to get the most out of a common-sense approach. Going that touch wider into the first jump will give you just a little more room and time across the middle to organize your line and your instructions to the horse. Use your head, work out the best route in the circumstances, and practise riding it. Your horse will let you know if you have got it wrong!

Take it gently. However good your horse is, do not do too much of this particular exercise. It is quite difficult to do well and rather stressful, both physically and mentally. Intersperse the tricky kinds of approaches with more straightforward doubles across the square. Practise reducing the number of strides taken on the loops, and only occasionally insert the more awkward approaches on your track.

This grid is ideal for practising with both novice and advanced horses.

If you get anything wrong, it will probably be because you have been too slow with your plans, and/or with your instructions. This grid will sharpen you up, so use it!

FIFTEEN

Related Distances

Gridwork can be very useful in solving specific problems, and one of the most common problems to be found in showjumping is getting the related distances right.

As far as the course builder is concerned, a normal showjumping stride is approximately 3.7m (12ft) in length, and all his combinations and related distances are measured with that presumption.

Conventional Measurement

The BSJA rulebook stipulates the distances to be set in combinations at affiliated shows, and most unaffiliated shows use these measurements as a guideline too. The minimum distance allowed for one stride between fences is 6.85m (22ft 6in), which is very short for a horse. The more common distance used is at least 30cm (1ft) longer. The maximum distance allowed for one stride to a spread jump is 7.5m (24ft 6in). If the second jump is an upright, the distance can be a little longer, to a maximum length of 8m (26ft 3in).

Once these distances have been set, they will be the same for all the competitors in the class, and in horse classes the size of the horses will range from 14.3hh to 17hh plus. It is clear that the smaller horses might have to stretch a bit, while the larger or longer-striding animals will have the opposite problem and must be taught to shorten their strides correspondingly.

A naturally short-striding horse has many advantages. He will be able to 'fiddle' his stride more easily than a longer-striding animal. If the rider gets in a muddle, he will find it simpler to pop in a short stride and still jump out of trouble. On the other hand, in a longish combination he will find the distance very difficult.

Lengthening the Stride

How can you encourage the horse to lengthen, remain active and jump out cleanly? With gridwork!

Carefully measure the distance required. 7.5m (24ft 6in) is a sensible length to start with, as it is the most common distance for one stride that you will find at shows. Build your grid with a double cross to a single cross to a single cross on this distance. Pop through the grid and just try to analyze what is happening underneath you. Is the horse landing and doing one normal stride and a short little propped effort? Or is he doing one normal stride and then producing huge leaps over the second and third jumps?

Keep the second and third fences as

single crosses. Until you have learned how to lengthen the stride and cope with conventional distances easily, you must avoid spreads. If your horse is finding it difficult to reach, it will severely dent his confidence if he keeps coming down on a back pole and hurting himself. This is a sure way to encourage refusals.

Put down six canter poles at 3m (10ft) intervals. If your horse is short striding, you will find that he will negotiate the poles easily with no loss of rhythm. Move the poles out to 3.35m (11ft) intervals. Is he starting to struggle? Towards the end of the line, is he landing a little short, not quite in the middle of the gaps?

You should feel if he is trailing slightly and not quite keeping the same rhythm. If you are still fine, it should be relatively easy to get him producing the 30cm (1ft) longer stride necessary to cope with the recommended distance of 7.5m (24ft 6in). If you are *not* fine, you must work over this line with more leg until he lengthens from behind into your hand. Do not go any faster. You will not get it right by going faster. Initially it might help him through the poles more successfully, but a jump from that extra pace would only be long, flat and careless. You have got to produce more impulsion.

Once you have managed to keep him going down the line without flagging, move the poles again to give you a length of 3.7m (12ft). If he really finds it difficult to land in the middle of the distance each time, you are going to have to do some strenuous gridwork. It is up to you to produce enough impulsion to enable him to lengthen his stride when he needs to most of all – in the middle of combinations.

However nimble he is, it would be an exceptionally agile horse that could consistently jump cleanly through a conventional one-stride combination taking two short strides. As the jumps get bigger, a limited stride will cause even more trouble. None of the other alternatives is at all attractive: enormous unbalanced leaps, getting too close to the jump and causing knockdowns, or refusals.

Go back to the grid and shorten the distances to the length he can cope with more easily; around 6.7m (22ft) will encourage him through the course without struggling or putting in extra strides. Put a placing pole exactly in the middle of each distance (Fig 31). Build the grid into a small parallel to small upright to small upright. The parallel will help the horse get in a little deeper. The next two upright jumps should then be fairly straightforward, with nothing very big. You are working at the moment to improve your horse's stride length, not his ability in the air.

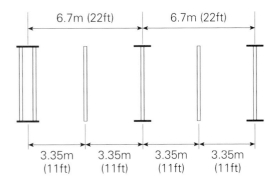

Once the horse is happily popping through the grid, move the first placing pole and the middle jump out by 30cm (1ft). Make the same distances with the second pole and last jump. The grid will run: small parallel to pole on 3.7m (12ft), to upright on 3.35m (11ft), to

Fig 31

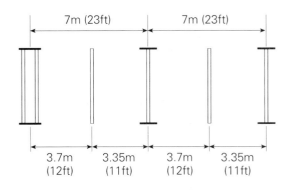

Fig 32

pole on 3.7m (12ft), to the last upright on 3.35m (11ft), as in Fig 32. See how your horse copes with this. If you land with your leg on and ride the pole properly from an 'up' position, he should lengthen his stride slightly. Although the distance between the jumps has increased, the pole should encourage the take-off point to remain the same. It will still be the same distance away from the uprights as before.

If the horse does not get the idea after four or five tries, shorten the distance by 15cm (6in) and prepare to move the poles and jumps by centimetres (inches) only. It might take longer to get there, but it is the simplest way to help him.

Do not feel you must do all this in only one session. If you plan to work on it for several days, you will not be pressurized into doing too much too

soon. It must be a gradual process in improving the horse's technique, or he will lose confidence. After all, when he approaches a double he does not think that he must try harder and lengthen his stride in case he cannot reach the second part. All he will think is that it is a long stretch and very hard work to get out again with no damage done. He will not reason it out that if he makes a longer stride, he will find the combination easy. He will actually be in there before he finds it difficult, and if he finds it too uncomfortable, he is going to view two or three jumps close together with suspicion and will be even less willing to stride in boldly with enough impulsion to help him through.

It is up to you to produce the horse's stride so that he will find it *easy*. Be patient. However long it takes, gradually change over the placing poles and second and third jumps. Do not consider any alterations until you are both totally happy with the distance you are doing. You will eventually end up with parallel to pole on 4m (13ft) to upright still on 3.35m (11ft), to pole on 4m (13ft) to last jump on 3.35m (11ft), as in Fig 33. The whole idea is to land and immediately produce enough impulsion and power to elevate and lengthen the whole stride. Working over the placing pole will help him reach the most beneficial take-off point for the second and third parts comfortably.

At a show, you will not have any scope for error. You must get your homework done thoroughly so that you can produce that lengthened stride every time. However talented and careful the short-striding horse is, you must help him. On a one-stride distance, he will not be able consistently to get in two strides accurately. He might just get

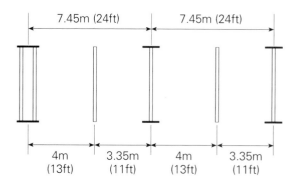

Fig 33

away with it in a double, but in a treble combination, there is bound to be a loss of impulsion. It will then be virtually impossible for him to jump through cleanly and comfortably taking either two strides or doing enormous leaps to compensate for not making up the ground.

Extra pace alone will not work. Obviously if you go in a bit faster, it will help to lengthen the stride slightly, simply through having more speed, but it certainly will not encourage the horse to jump cleanly. You must get impulsion. If you have increased the pace, the middle stride will be fast, long and flat, and will only encourage the horse to be careless, almost from a sense of desperation, which he is picking up from you. You might even be engineering a stop, because he will think he cannot make it.

For any success in the ring, you must help your horse to produce up-tempo, rounded, bouncy strides – strides that cover the ground with impulsion and power. The grid will help you get that feel, and you must reproduce it yourself when you leave the grid. Do not just sit there as a passenger and expect the poles to do all the work for you. You will not find them in the ring.

Quick reactions

As soon as you land, sharpen up your reactions. Get your body as quickly as possible into an 'up' position and use lots of leg. Make sure you do not throw your hands forward to urge the stride: only your leg will be able to do that.

The quicker you can apply the aids after landing, the better chance you have of lengthening your horse's stride. Do all the usual things, but even sharper than normal. Look up, keep a good contact and do not go with your body to the second and third jumps. The poles will most certainly help the stride because you will both have something to aim at in the middle. Then, once you have actually produced the right feel and your horse is no longer struggling, remove the placing poles. Do not throw away the feeling they produced.

Your reactions should be sharpened! Your balance must be 'just so' as quickly as possible after landing so that your instructions are given rapidly. Tell your horse to lengthen by giving him the correct signals *immediately*, and keep producing a similar quick application of the aids so that he does not relax and shorten again. He will not know that lengthening is making it easier for him to jump. All he will understand is that if he responds to your quicker and much more positive aids, then his job is far more straightforward.

Condensing the Stride

Small and short-striding horses are not the only ones to find the recommended distances awkward. Sometimes horses just make up too much ground in the air, and find themselves too close for comfort to the second or third elements in a combination, or their legs are long and they find a conventional 3.7m (12ft) stride often a little difficult to produce consistently. This exercise, more or less in reverse, will help them too.

Again start off with canter poles that suit the horse's stride exactly. You might find some horses needing a stride as long as 4.3m (14ft) to be quite comfortable. Gradually reduce the distances until you are back to 3.7m (12ft). You might find it hard work to hold enough to shorten him up, but do not forget your leg. If

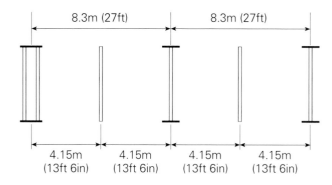

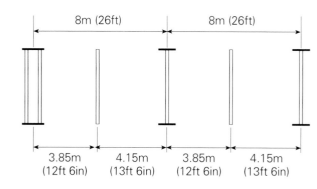

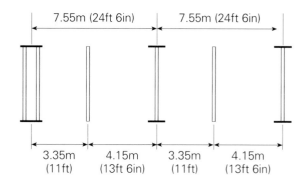

*Fig 34 Condensing
the stride.*

your contact is too strong without enough leg you will only slow him down, not producing a light, bouncy stride.

Once you have him working happily through the poles and landing in the middle of the distances, try him on the grid. Use the same jumps and start the distances at 8.3m (27ft), with placing poles in the middle.

As you *gradually* shorten the distance to the conventional 7.45–7.7m (24–25ft), move the placing poles correspondingly closer to the landing sides of the first and second jump. The poles should help prevent the horse bounding through and getting far too close to the second and third jumps. They will help him shorten his stride as he lands, giving you an opportunity to steady and produce the necessary impulsion without having to overcheck. He will lose accuracy if he simply makes up too much ground, so you have got to help him.

Practise acquiring the feel the placing poles are giving you as your horse lands. Do not lose your contact in the air. You must be sharp to gather him up. Keep your weight well behind his shoulder and deeply down into the stirrup; do not let him be too quick for you and lug you forward out of balance. If he lands and leaps forward he will make up too much ground, and there will be no time or room to get up cleanly; if he lands and lengthens he will not have time and room to get up either. He *must* be asked to land and shorten. Only then will you be able to hold him off the next jump so that he can be accurate.

This type of grid will help both long- and short-striding horses. Accuracy with the distances and careful placing of the ground poles will assure improvement. You will be able to feel how it should be to jump your combinations well. The tricky bit is when you remove the poles.

Have you practised enough to be able to reproduce the conventional striding with nothing to help you?

If you find the stride begins to deteriorate, go back to the grid and work some more. Unless you use the grid to improve the general swiftness of your instructions, your horse will not shorten or lengthen as required. You do not need to ride better; you do not have to improve your style – you just need sharper reactions. You must be able to land in balance well enough to produce stride one properly. In a 7.45m (24ft) combination, it is the only stride you've got, so there is no margin for error.

SIXTEEN

Cross-country Benefits

Below and opposite: A grid of relatively small but carefully positioned horizontal bounces help Samantha and Josh to practise producing the necessary impulsion required to tackle a steep set of steps.

Note the similarity in the activity produced by the hind leg for both grid and steps.

Cross country is a much safer and more enjoyable pastime if your horse has been well brought up over his grids. He will be neat, nimble and active; grids will teach him to rely on being able to use his scope and ability if things go wrong and a potential disaster is looming.

Bounce fences and steps are particular areas where the grid will help you both. A bounce grid, set on a shortish distance of 3–3.35m (10–11ft) will help you both

practise the rhythm of producing a jumping effort from every touchdown. Practise the short distance. When you are out on a course you will be going faster, and the speed will make up the extra ground that a correct cross-country bounce will be set, around 3.7–4.3m (12–14ft).

However fast you are going, you will still need impulsion to keep active on every stride. The grid will provide you

1

2

3

4

Note the similarity in the activity produced by the hind leg for both grid and steps.

with the practice to do this while still staying in balance. You should be working for impulsion and balance on every stride, but it will be absolutely vital to be 100 per cent active for uphill steps and banks. If you are not sharp to balance immediately after jumping up on to a bank, you will certainly come off in a heap with no control and no steering.

Although hitting fences on your cross-country rounds remains unpenalised, obviously it will be much safer if your horse tries to clear them. Combination obstacles are now fairly commonplace, and your horse will need all the skills of a showjumper to produce active strides and clean jumping. The square grid (Chapter 14), the steering grid (Chapter 13), and the jump-off exercises (Chapter 12) will help you to produce accurate lines over the angled jumps and corners that catch out so many riders. The more practised you are with the directional controls, the less likely you will be to have glance-offs.

The grids with high crosses to help horses back off and jump cleanly at speed (Chapter 11) are also ideal for cross-country practice. It will be very comforting to know that your horse can stay clean if you approach a fence a little bit faster than intended.

If there is something tricky or spooky on the course that your horse may not like, the gridwork for naughty horses (Chapters 5 and 6) will make you sharp to interpret his signals, and even sharper to get your leg on strongly enough to avoid a refusal.

Many water complexes nowadays have their own bounce approaches or exits. The gridwork over short bounces will help your balance to be in the right position to drive your horse on if he is a little reluctant. The same applies to ditches, particularly trakehners. The grid will give you enough expertise to recognize just how quickly to act and how much leg to use to maintain a good rhythm on your approach. Even if there is a slight hesitation, as long as you are hanging well in balance you will be able to keep your horse going. With fixed fences to negotiate, any way of minimizing the risk is well worth the effort involved.

Whatever you want to jump, gridwork will help you jump it better!

SEVENTEEN

Advanced Horses

When a horse is experienced, he will need little jumping work at home to keep him tuned up between competitions. If he starts to get careless after going consistently well, it will probably be because you have both become a little complacent.

Maybe your leg has got a touch lazy and you are failing to produce quite enough impulsion to get him to come up cleanly. When a nice horse knows his job well, he will perform to the best of his ability without any problems and it is then very easy for the rider to become quite slovenly and to relax the pressure of producing the horse with maximum impulsion. If an experienced horse taps an odd pole, it is usually because he has not been helped enough by the rider. He will be lacking impulsion because the rider has eased up on the aids and failed to keep producing the activity necessary from the hind leg. The rider is leaving it too much to the horse.

Perhaps the horse has become a little uncooperative, and is leaning on the forehand. The rider will then find it much more difficult to get the correct degree of balance between hand and leg to keep him light.

Whatever the cause, you need some help to put the horse in a position where you can sharpen him up and keep him consistently at competition level.

Variations with Conventional Grids

A time or two down some shortish horizontal bounces will usually be all you need to get the horse's eye in. It will lighten him up in front and give you the chance to produce more power from your leg. Do not forget to scold him if you hear him tapping his toes. Being experienced, he will probably find this work easy, and it may not wake him up quite enough to be prepared to make more effort.

Try the square grid. The different twists and turns you can ride will keep your horse on his toes, but it might not encourage him to make more effort over the poles. If he is starting to be a touch careless in the ring, and these exercises are not encouraging him to make more effort, build a long grid: parallel to upright to upright to parallel on 7.45–7.7m (24–25ft) distances. Jump through it several times, gradually building it up to whatever height you are jumping in the ring.

Now what is he being too relaxed with? Add a surprise. Whichever jump he is too casual with, place a block or a cone underneath it. Putting in high crosses will make little difference to an experienced horse. He has seen plenty of them in his career, so they will not hold any additional attention-grabbing value for him. He knows too much to treat them with anything but indifference.

Even a very experienced horse will notice the difference a cone makes, and it will make him drop his nose and concentrate; then you can get more leg on without him pulling your arms out, as it will stop him leaning on you and lugging you forward out of balance. You will be in a position to increase his activity, and stop being the passenger that perhaps caused the whole lack of impulsion in the first place!

Even if you are sure you have not been slack, you still have to do something to get the horse going well again. It is usually only a bit of boredom that causes the problem *if* the horse is at fault. Horses with a lot of ability find the work easy and can manage to get by using only three-quarters effort. If you start to relax, the horse will pick up on it and not make so much effort himself.

When your horse keeps jumping consistently well, there will come a point when you forget *why*. It is only because you keep producing impulsion. The second you ease up on insisting for maximum effort, so will he. Why should he just carry a passenger? It is meant to be a partnership.

This grid will help you rediscover the correct degree of impulsion required *all* the time. However easy he has found it, the addition of a 'foreign body' in the middle somewhere will make him peek. It would be a very wooden and dull horse who did not notice the difference and back off the tiniest touch into your hand. This is the split second you should be waiting for. The cone will give you the chance to instantaneously put more leg on and it *will* produce a much cleaner, higher jump by producing far more of an effort.

Keep changing the position of the cone, first under one jump, then under a different one in the line. Use two cones or an old filler if you have to, but get him paying attention. This is an experienced horse, not a novice – keep him on his toes. Certainly he will not be frightened, but he will be more alert. It is almost the same principle as using a bright pole in a plain grid when you are trying to correct naughty horses from stopping. The feel you get is the one you want to recapture in the ring.

Is your attitude correct? You need to be riding your horse all the time. He has probably only become slightly blasé because he has picked it up from you. Do not let it happen to a nice horse. It will stem from your attitude, not your riding ability.

You know how quickly the horse will sense how you feel. If your attitude is quite brisk and workmanlike, the small bounces should be all that is necessary to tune up and reaffirm his accuracy. If your attitude has become a bit casual, your horse will pick it up too. Practise over this spooky type of grid to get you both in tune to work together again. It has to come from you. He is a good horse, and you want him to remain so, so keep your riding ability and your attitude constantly under review.

Advanced Grids

Diagonal poles through a grid will also encourage an experienced horse to concentrate and take notice. Try a grid of St Andrew's cross to three alternate small diagonal poles to another St Andrew's cross all placed on the bounce distance of 3.7m (12ft). This grid will look very complicated as you approach and it will require effort to jump through cleanly. Scold him if he does not.

Just make sure you steer him through the middle. Do not let him learn to snake from side to side to jump the middle bounce jumps more easily where they are lower. A very bright horse will always try to! Alternate the three small diagonals in the middle from the back pole of the first cross. As you carry on alternating, the end crosses will be differently slanted at the front from the first cross.

If you have been experiencing slight problems with a particular front leg, add another diagonal bounce in the middle. As the poles are now alternating, the first and last jumps will be identical in appearance. Build your grid so that the first pole of each cross is slanted so that the high side is towards the dangly leg. It will then give you two jumps on the grid specifically designed to help you. You will not need to change it round to come the other way. With four diagonal bounce poles, the crosses in reverse will still be on the correct slant to help the lazy leg. If you like, you can also raise the high side of the two relevant diagonal poles to help as well, but you must be able to steer straight down the middle.

If there is no particular side to correct, three poles will be plenty. The jumbled appearance of the grid will make the horse look and be prepared to listen. Even more important, it will give you a chance to put more leg on to recapture the 100 per cent impulsion.

Special Problems

Once you have plenty of experience in the ring, you might find that there is one particular fence bothering you. Put it in the grid.

Some types of rider only need to hit a particular fence twice to develop a phobia. Instead of coming into the disliked jump on a good rhythm and totally ignoring what type of jump it is, they either override too strongly or flap and fiddle, so of course they will have it down. The horse wonders what is wrong as the rider changes style, and he starts to anticipate trouble. It is a very easy vicious circle for you both to get into.

Planks can often cause trouble purely because they are very stark and look unforgiving. Build a grid of parallel to upright to parallel on the distance that your horse prefers. Deliberately set yourself up with a perfect stride and have the planks in the middle, quite low to begin with. The third jump is there to ensure that you keep riding after the bogey fence.

The perfect-distance approach should help: you will *know* that you are not going to meet the planks awkwardly. If you have been panicking and chasing into them, you should be able to calm down and not distract your horse. Now try to ride the planks as if they were your favourite sort of fence – not easy! You will meet the planks perfectly and he should treat them as if they were any other upright fence; try to do the same.

If you are sure that it is not your problem and he is still careless, the problem will probably be with the front legs. Lengthen the distance by a metre (yard), and put a pole on the ground the same distance in front of the planks. This will give him just a little more time and room to snap up. Do not forget to ride away after the planks, or you will start to be careless at something else. Use the same method to keep him jumping cleanly over a gate, another stark upright that seems to invite further problems.

Triple bars are another jump that the rider may misjudge, again because she might not like the look of them. It is very easy to try to get a bit more pace into a wider jump, but if you jump it correctly you will be able to minimize the spread. Standing off a long way is unwise, so set the triple bar in the middle of the grid on a metre (yard) shorter distance than normal. You want to get the horse right into the bottom of the fence to cut down the spread. You will be able to do this with a staircase type of jump, as the shape of the fence accommodates the natural parabola of a nice rounded leap. Practise on the grid until you are happy with the approach. The last jump will make sure that you are not sloppy in the air because there will still be work to do.

Check your timing, and that it is not simply a shift of your weight bringing his toe down on the back pole. This is a very easy fence to mistime. You are airborne perhaps longer than you will have allowed for in your balance and this could be the reason why sometimes you do not quite make the spread, so use the exercise to make sure it is not your timing that is out.

You will not normally see triple bars in the middle or end of combinations. The BSJA rule book excludes them from this position in novice classes, but in a grid with the sole purpose of producing a better stride it is quite acceptable to use them in the middle. Be familiar with the length of stride of your horse, and do not set an impossible task. If he is touching with his front legs, extend the room allowed. If he is catching with his hind legs, shorten up the distance slightly. Often an adjustment of just a few centimetres (inches) will be enough to change the whole aspect of the exercise and give you enough confidence to maintain the required improvement.

There are no limits to how gridwork will help both you and your horse improve your jumping, so do it!

Above:
Charlie and Mary brush up their technique so that they stay accurate at this uninviting obstacle.

Opposite, top:
Barney is being careless at the planks, as usual!

Opposite, bottom:
Moving the placing pole slightly towards the first jump gives Amanda more chance to hold Barney off the planks and produce a cleaner jump. Then she must reproduce the same feeling without the help of the poles!

Index